UNDER THE SWASTIKA
IN NAZI GERMANY

German History in Focus

Series Editors

Lisa Pine, London South Bank University, UK
Peter C. Caldwell, Rice University, USA

Editorial Advisory Board

Benjamin Marschke, Humboldt State University, USA
Monica Black, University of Tennessee, Knoxville, USA
Matthew Jefferies, University of Manchester, UK
Neil Gregor, University of Southampton, UK
Christina Morina, Bielefeld University, Germany
Joachim Whaley, University of Cambridge, UK
Bridget Heal, University of St. Andrews, UK

Published Titles

Under the Swastika in Nazi Germany, Kristin Semmens

Upcoming Titles

Germany in the Central Middle Ages, Johanna Dale
The Weimar Republic: A Democracy, Christopher Dillon
A Nation on the Move: Germany 1815–1871, Jasper Heinzen
Imperial Germany: The History of an Empire, Kenneth Ledford
The Empire's Reformation: Politics and Religion in Germany,
1495–1648, David Luebke
The German Democratic Republic: A Short History,
Ned Richardson-Little
West Germany in Focus, Julia Sneeringer

UNDER THE SWASTIKA
IN NAZI GERMANY

Kristin Semmens

BLOOMSBURY ACADEMIC
LONDON • NEW YORK • OXFORD • NEW DELHI • SYDNEY

BLOOMSBURY ACADEMIC
Bloomsbury Publishing Plc
50 Bedford Square, London, WC1B 3DP, UK
1385 Broadway, New York, NY 10018, USA
29 Earlsfort Terrace, Dublin 2, Ireland

BLOOMSBURY, BLOOMSBURY ACADEMIC and the Diana logo are
trademarks of Bloomsbury Publishing Plc

First published in Great Britain 2022

Copyright © Kristin Semmens, 2022

Kristin Semmens has asserted their right under the Copyright, Designs and
Patents Act, 1988, to be identified as Author of this work.

Series design by Toby Way
Cover image: A young woman in the Sudetenland region of Czechoslovakia
places swastika flags around a portrait of Nazi leader Adolf Hitler in
anticipation of the arrival of German troops, 30 September 1938.
(Photo by Becke/FPG/Hulton Archive/Getty Images)

Bloomsbury Publishing Plc does not have any control over, or responsibility
for, any third-party websites referred to or in this book. All internet addresses
given in this book were correct at the time of going to press. The author and
publisher regret any inconvenience caused if addresses have changed or sites
have ceased to exist, but can accept no responsibility for any such changes.

Every effort has been made to trace the copyright holders and obtain
permission to reproduce the copyright material. Please do get in touch with
any enquiries or any information relating to such material or the rights holder.
We would be pleased to rectify any omissions in subsequent editions of this
publication should they be drawn to our attention.

A catalogue record for this book is available from the British Library.

A catalog record for this book is available from the Library of Congress.

ISBN: HB: 978-1-3501-4280-0
PB: 978-1-3501-4279-4
ePDF: 978-1-3501-4281-7
eBook: 978-1-3501-4282-4

Typeset by Newgen KnowledgeWorks Pvt. Ltd., Chennai, India
Printed and bound in Great Britain

To find out more about our authors and books visit www.bloomsbury.com
and sign up for our newsletters.

CONTENTS

FIGURES

MAPS

SERIES EDITORS' PREFACE

This series introduces the main eras of German history since the Middle Ages in a short, easily surveyable, and focused way. Its aim is to provide readers with an overview that is digestible for students, that offers teachers a point from which they can jump off into more complex topics, and that includes useful starting points for further research. The books in the series organize material in a way that gets to the crux of each period, written in an engaging and informative style. The volumes cover essential periods in German history, from medieval to contemporary history. Each book examines political life, the economy, society and cultural life during a specific period of German history. The focused approach allows subject experts to analyse a significant topic in a way that sheds light, particularly for a student audience, on the key or essential aspects of the history of each era. The series offers a fresh and up-to-date insight into many aspects of German history that either have not been approached in this way, or perhaps more significantly, have not been treated recently. The series gives an English-language readership access to the most recent developments in the field, including scholarship in German. Within each volume, readers will be able to understand the essence of the period in the volume, which, as the series title suggests, is brought into clear and sharp focus by each of our authors.

Lisa Pine and Peter C. Caldwell

PREFACE

This is a book about Germans in Nazi Germany. It begins on 30 January 1933, when Adolf Hitler became Chancellor, and ends on 9 May 1945, the date of Germany's unconditional surrender in the Second World War. The story it tells is organized into five successive phases and told from the perspective of five different categories of Germans. To understand the varied experiences of German insiders and outsiders in these twelve years, historians have long used the triad of perpetrators, victims and bystanders. The fivefold classification scheme proposed by this book – Nazis, accomplices, supporters, racial and social outsiders, resisters – provides a new framework for understanding Germans' responses to, and engagement with, National Socialism, which better captures the complexity of life under Hitler. These categories also closely mirror perceptions at the time: Nazi ideology and practice configured Germans as prime movers, collaborative partners and upholders of the regime or as its outcasts and opponents. While traditional identities – based mainly on class, region and religion – did not disappear under Hitler, what overwhelmingly determined lived experience was how individuals and social groups were situated in relation to the Nazi regime, whether by choice or by imposition. This book's structure reflects that reality, which was profoundly shaped by Nazi ambitions for German society.

The Third Reich was an aggressively expansionist regime, which committed many of its most brutal crimes on foreign soil against millions of non-Germans. Those imperialist dynamics are central to understanding it, but *Under the Swastika in Nazi Germany* focuses on Germans 'at home'. It examines their actions, experiences and attitudes and shows how these changed over time between 1933 and 1945. Each of the five chapters incorporates major political, economic, social and cultural events and pinpoints key shifts in the nature and goals of

Hitler's regime. This provides the vital context for understanding the diversity of Germans' responses to it, and how, in turn, those responses shaped the regime itself. The goal is an integrated history, which includes Hitler and his henchmen but highlights the interrelatedness and interdependence of a broader range of German lives.[1] The stories about insiders and outsiders told here overlap and intersect, even as they collide, reflecting the interactions historical actors had with each other. By presenting them together, the book offers multiple, complementary perspectives on Nazi Germany. For more information on the range of issues raised, readers are encouraged to consult the suggestions for further reading.

ACKNOWLEDGEMENTS

Holocaust survivor and author Elie Wiesel once noted the similarities between writing and sculpture, whereby words are removed, just as stone is chiselled away, to reveal the final work. I am very grateful to those who assisted me with the removal process, especially to my colleague, mentor and friend, Tom Saunders, for suggestions on how to pare down the original, much longer manuscript. Thank you to my students at the University of Victoria, Canada, whose questions have honed my thinking about Nazi Germany over two decades. Aaron Gelmon, Katie Bentley and Kästle van der Meer merit special mention. I am lucky to have many encouraging friends, including Anneke de Rudder and Kimberley Rogers, who read earlier drafts, and a sister, Jessica Larouche, who is a meticulous proofreader. My editorial team at Bloomsbury, especially Rhodri Mogford and Laura Reeves, and the *German History in Focus* series editors, Peter C. Caldwell and Lisa Pine, offered invaluable support. Additional thanks go to the two anonymous reviewers whose critiques and advice made this a better book. My parents, Monika and Ted Semmens, read every word of multiple versions and gave empathetic criticism. Finally, thank you to my husband, Derek Little, and my children, Annika Little and Turner Little, who listened patiently to stories I had to omit but still wanted to tell.

GLOSSARY OF ABBREVIATIONS AND TERMS

Abwehr	Military Intelligence Organization
Anschluss	union with Austria
BDM	League of German Girls
Blitzkrieg	lightning war
DAF	German Labour Front
Führer	Leader
Gestapo	Secret State Police
Gleichschaltung	coordination
Gauleiter	Regional Leader
Kapo	prisoner functionary
Kreisleiter	District Leader
Kristallnacht	November pogrom, 9–10 November 1938
Lebensraum	living space
Luftwaffe	Air Force
Mittelstand	lower-middle class
NSDAP	National Socialist German Workers Party (i.e. Nazi Party)
Putsch	coup
Reichstag	Parliament
Reich	Empire
SA	Storm Division (i.e. Stormtroopers or Brownshirts)
SOPADE	Social Democratic Party of Germany in Exile
SS	Protection Squad
Volk	people
Volksgemeinschaft	people's community
Volkssturm	People's Storm militia
Waffen-SS	Armed SS
Wehrmacht	Armed Forces; until 1935, Reichswehr

INTRODUCTION: THE NAZI RISE TO POWER

The immediate roots of National Socialism can be traced to Germany's military defeat in the First World War and the political revolution that followed, which launched the country's first experiment with genuine democracy, the Weimar Republic. As the war ended in autumn 1918, Germany was in turmoil. Almost 1,775,000 German soldiers had died, most in the trenches that stretched along the Western Front. An Allied blockade meant starvation for some and hunger for many. Soldiers and sailors mutinied, refusing their commanders' last, desperate orders. Some formed councils alongside German workers calling for revolution. No mass uprising occurred, but an intensely war-weary population demanded change. The Emperor, Kaiser Wilhelm II, abdicated on 9 November 1918, and was replaced by a council of left-wing Social Democrats. Two days later, the guns fell silent when German and French representatives signed an armistice. Elections in January 1919 installed the first of many coalition governments, eventually representing almost the full spectrum of political parties. That spectrum ranged from the right-wing German National People's Party, hostile opponents of democracy who desired the return of the old order, to the far left Communist Party, which dreamt of a Bolshevik-style revolution like Russia's in 1917. On 28 June 1919, German representatives signed the infamous and punitive Treaty of Versailles. Germany lost its colonies, 10 per cent of its European territory (plus 13 per cent of its population) and saw its armed forces reduced to 100,000 men. The Rhineland, an area along the western border with France, was stripped of any German military presence. Saddled with responsibility for the war, Germany also had to pay enormous reparations to the Allies for wartime damages.

Outraged and humiliated, many Germans were receptive to popular slogans that fundamentally misrepresented their situation. Brave German soldiers defending the Fatherland were, according to the myth, 'stabbed in the back' by disloyal civilians, including Jews, communists and socialists, alongside supposed swindlers and defeatists. Some proponents of the myth also blamed these groups for the new democratic political system, which seemed to lurch from disaster to disaster: first a hyperinflation crisis in 1923 and then the Great Depression, which saw over six million unemployed by 1932. Many Germans were shocked as well by Weimar's experimental avant-garde culture. Radical solutions offered by extremist political parties fell on increasingly fertile ground. The Communist Party tripled its membership by 1932. Yet far more successful was a once obscure, Bavarian-based movement, the National Socialist German Workers Party (NSDAP), known as the Nazi Party. Its leader (*Führer*) was an Austrian who fought for Germany in the Great War and had been briefly imprisoned following a failed *putsch* attempt in Munich in 1923. His name was Adolf Hitler.

Adolf Hitler

Adolf Hitler (1889–1945) was born in the Austrian village of Braunau am Inn, bordering Germany. After failing to gain entry to the Academy of Fine Arts in Vienna – he had some talents as a painter – he moved to Munich (Germany). When the First World War broke out, Hitler enlisted in a German regiment and served on the Western Front. He returned to Munich after the war, where he joined the far-right German Workers Party. He was an effective speaker and was quickly put in charge of party propaganda. He also designed their black, white and red flag featuring a swastika – rotated 45 degrees – at its centre. An ancient religious symbol of peace and well-being now stood for hatred and 'Aryan' supremacy. By 1921, Hitler was chairman of the renamed National Socialist German Workers Party (Nazi Party). On 9 November 1923, he and 2,000 supporters staged the Beer Hall Putsch, a failed attempt to gain control over the Bavarian state. He served a nine-month prison sentence for treason, during which he began writing his political manifesto, *My Struggle* (*Mein Kampf*). After his release, Hitler worked doggedly to rebuild the Nazi Party and eventually achieved spectacular success at the polls in the early 1930s. By the end of 1932, as the Nazi movement's unchallenged leader (*Führer*), Hitler was poised to lead what he viewed as Germany's national and racial struggle.

The Nazi Party leapt from 2.8 per cent of the popular vote in the 1928 federal election to over 33 per cent in two 1932 elections. The Nazis now had support in districts across the country and among an exceptionally diverse electorate. Although head of the largest party in parliament (*Reichstag*), Hitler was distrusted; conservative power brokers denied him the chancellorship. Yet wanting to exploit his popularity for their own purposes and seeing no other options, these figures, led by the German President, Paul von Hindenburg, and former Chancellor Franz von Papen, soon bowed to Hitler's demands to be Chancellor. On 30 January 1933, they appointed him to lead a new coalition of Nazis and conservatives.

What did Hitler and his National Socialists want? Chief among the Nazis' ambitions, deeply rooted in Hitler's own ideology, were ending liberal democracy and exterminating leftist movements (socialism and communism), which they felt had weakened the strength of the German nation. Certain factions within the movement called for the eradication of capitalism's abuses and inequities. As diehard nationalists, the Nazis were also committed to making Germany great again. The humiliating Versailles Treaty, which had turned their country into a pariah on the world stage, had to be destroyed. Expansion and conquest of living space (*Lebensraum*) in Eastern Europe were required to feed a growing population. National survival made war necessary. Thus, war would have to come again. One social concept stood above all. Hitler envisioned an ideal *Volksgemeinschaft* (people's community). Those Germans belonging to it would no longer identify themselves by class, region or religion but as 'comrades' united by race and devotion to creating a greater Germany.

Volksgemeinschaft

One of the most central concepts of Nazi ideology, *Volksgemeinschaft* is variously translated as 'people's community', 'national community', 'racial community' and 'ethnic community'. Because Hitler's vision embraced all of those at once, this book uses the German word throughout. The imagined *Volksgemeinschaft* was to be a racially pure, harmonious community uniting all Germans in devotion to their people, their nation and, of course, their leader. A popular Nazi slogan summed up the idea: *'Ein Volk! Ein Reich! Ein Führer!'* (One People! One Empire! One Leader!). At the same time, the *Volksgemeinschaft* excluded all people deemed to be harmful to that community.

All members of this homogenous 'Aryan' community – the term denoted a supposedly superior, ethnically pure Germanic race – would prosper, because all inner and external threats to its existence would be overcome. These included Jews, 'Gypsies' (Sinti and Roma) and other racial enemies, along with racially 'degenerate' and socially 'inferior' individuals, such as homosexuals, the disabled and so-called 'asocials'. Within this world view, hatred and hostility to Jews (antisemitism) were fundamental. Building on longstanding Christian animosity, compounded by nineteenth-century racial 'science', the Nazis planned to solve an imagined 'Jewish Question' by ending the Jews' alleged excessive, malignant influence on the German economy, society and culture.

'Asocials'

'Asocials' were people who deviated, in the Nazi view, from desired societal and behavioural norms. They included the homeless, beggars, prostitutes, juvenile offenders, the 'work shy' (people who 'refused' to work), those with addictions and criminal convictions, and pacifists (people who believe war is unjustified). Sinti and Roma Germans were regularly classified as 'asocial', as were lesbians.

Many Germans could believe in the vision of a *Volksgemeinschaft* and see it as a worthy goal without endorsing everything Hitler and the Nazis meant by it. Its pro-German positive attributes – a renewed nation, a strong, unified population – likely attracted more supporters than its negative ones based on the exclusion of, and discrimination against, others. While Nazism's violent antisemitic core certainly drew followers, most of the Germans who turned to the Nazis did so because they believed that only Hitler and his Party, through radical initiatives, could solve Weimar's crises of mass unemployment and political instability, counter the rising threat from the left and restore some kind of normality to daily life. The Nazis' violent language was often dismissed as belonging only to isolated extremists among them. None of this makes Hitler's ascent or hold on power after 1933 inevitable. Focusing on how Germans responded to the Nazi regime helps us to understand both.

The chapters that follow focus on five chronologically distinct phases within the lifespan of the Third Reich. Some are broadly familiar; one in particular, 1938–40, deviates from the conventional focus on 1939 as the year of transition from peace to war. Each chapter begins with a very brief narrative of key events in Germany, and later, within the growing German Reich. These narratives are intentionally top-down in perspective: what the Nazi regime and its leaders did in a particular period amid shifting domestic and international circumstances. Thereafter, the perspective is reversed. A bottom-up approach looks at how Germans were affected by, interpreted and responded to the events of that particular phase.

In a speech soon after becoming Chancellor, Hitler divided the inhabitants of Germany into two groups: 'us' versus 'them', supporters versus opponents, friends versus enemies, the fit versus the unfit, superior versus inferior. He contrasted those willing to fight with the Nazis 'for the resurrection' of the nation with those who 'sin[ned]' against it through their beliefs, behaviour or indeed their very being.[1] In other words, he separated people who belonged to the imagined *Volksgemeinschaft* from people condemned to remain outside it, by circumstance or choice. Historians of Nazi Germany employ many terms to reflect this understanding of fundamental social division, including the Nazis' own (for example, community 'comrades' and 'aliens'). This book contrasts insiders with outsiders, not only to avoid the constant repetition of Nazi language but also because these labels – whether consciously adopted or forced upon them – reflect the sense Germans had of themselves at the time. Some Germans recognized and desired the benefits and privileges open to them that came with belonging inside the *Volksgemeinschaft*; others suffered the undeniable consequences of being cast out.

For a number of reasons, however, this binary division does not adequately capture the complexity of lives under the swastika. First, insiders and outsiders were alike in being Germans, even if not in the eyes of the Nazi state. They were citizens of Germany when Hitler came to power and most thought of themselves as German. Second, the dividing line between them was not always clear-cut. Identities could overlap and coexist, as well as change over time. Third, there were significant differences among insiders and between outsiders. For all these reasons, a fivefold division more accurately reflects the varieties of lived experience. Three of these – Nazis, accomplices, supporters – represent the insiders; the other two – racial and social outsiders and resisters – comprise the outsiders.

The *Nazis* were those who explicitly aligned themselves with the new regime and by so doing committed themselves to its goals. They were the most active, fervent devotees of the Third Reich and this book reserves the term for these enthusiasts: Hitler and his henchmen, loyal activists in the Nazi Party, members of its paramilitary divisions (the SA and SS), and its main auxiliary and sponsored organizations, like the Hitler Youth and others. It does so while recognizing that Germans could share enthusiasm for Nazi aims and values without joining groups affiliated with the Nazi Party, and that, conversely, Germans could join the Party or its organizations for reasons beyond deep conviction, in order to conform, for example, or advance their career prospects.

Accomplices were predominantly the traditional, usually conservative, elites who played a central role in bringing Hitler to power and keeping him there by serving his aims, even when their political beliefs did not always align perfectly with National Socialism. They included high-ranking government ministers and top civil servants, military officers, judges, academics, scions of industry and landed estate owners. 'Accomplices' is a loaded but apt term to describe this group, indicating everything from responsibility for Hitler's appointment and the success of his regime to willingness to collaborate in its authoritarian, expansionist and murderous objectives. They are distinguished broadly from the German population as a whole by their influence, opportunities to act and direct participation in specific Nazi goals. With these came greater accountability for its crimes.

This book calls the largest group of insiders – the majority German population without direct political influence – *supporters*. These factory workers, farmers and employees, women and children, Catholics and Protestants, have been the subject of a vast scholarship since the 1980s, when the history of everyday life under Hitler emerged as an important field of study. Racially acceptable to the Nazis, 'ordinary' insiders could be more ambivalent about Nazism.[2] Yet generally they not only complied with but also identified with and applauded the general direction in which Hitler was steering Germany. The Third Reich was built on their tacit or explicit support.

Racial and social outsiders can be identified as the victims of Nazi persecution, violence and, ultimately, murder. They were banished from the imagined *Volksgemeinschaft* by ethnicity (Jewish, Sinti and Roma, and Black Germans), physical and intellectual 'fitness' (disabled Germans), behaviour (Germans deemed to be 'asocial') and political conviction (Germans who remained loyal to other ideologies and refused to accept the one-party state). They were not a homogenous group. Some the Nazis viewed as capable of possible 'rehabilitation' (e.g.

individual homosexuals or former socialists); others they perceived as being unredeemable for the nation. Some political opponents who stayed in Germany, and who were not killed immediately or consigned to concentration camps in revenge, managed to live inconspicuously and avoided becoming targets of persecution. That demanded at least outward conformity, even if inwardly, they felt like outsiders in the new Germany. That option was not available to other Germans. The sections of this book on those racial and social outsiders trace the genesis and realization of the Holocaust (the mass murder of European Jews) as well as the experiences of other victims of genocide.

Resisters are the other group among outsiders, Germans who actively opposed the Nazi regime. Since 1945, historians have struggled to define what constituted resistance to Hitler and how to distinguish it clearly from expression of disapproval, dissent or disobedience. As we shall see, many otherwise supportive or at least compliant Germans found fault with certain aspects of the Third Reich and behaved in ways that could bring serious consequences. However, the sections on resisters in this book do not concentrate on everyday nonconformity, such as grumbling or joking, though they do point out significant examples. They focus on Germans who challenged the regime and rejected it based on political, religious or moral principles. These included communists, socialists, Christians and, much later, conservative elites, as well as opponents of specific policies. The definition of what qualifies as resistance is much broader for racially and socially excluded victims, in recognition of just how narrow their horizon of possibilities was. These sections therefore include a variety of forms of cultural and spiritual resistance, as well as actions that attempted to limit or end the oppressors' power and that opposed the Nazis' acts, policies and intentions. These included strategies to reduce suffering and make survival possible.

Chapter 1, Beginnings (1933–1935), sets the stage for what follows by introducing key individuals and organizations, and the foundational aspects of Nazi Germany, including its initial repression and racialized violence. After the storms of 1933–5 came the norms that are the subject of Chapter 2, The 'Good Old Days' (1936–1937). For many insiders, these were the most stable and happiest years of the Third Reich. For outsiders, though never normal, they were often relatively calm. From vastly different perspectives, these were better times than those that followed.

Chapter 3, Victory and Persecution (1938–1940), highlights 1938 as a transformative year for Germans, albeit in vastly different ways for different groups. It contrasts the intensified assault on outsiders – including the violent pogrom launched against Jews in November 1938 and the murders of disabled Germans – with insiders' growing acclamation for Hitler's successful territorial expansion. It also reveals how the outbreak of war in 1939, and subsequent military victories, profoundly affected society. Chapter 4, Descent (1941–1943), addresses the early German defeats and the turn to 'total war'. Conditions now deteriorated dramatically for German soldiers and the home front, while the fate of the Jews in Germany was sealed with the implementation of systematic extermination, known as the 'Final Solution'. Chapter 5, The End (1944–1945), recounts how Germans responded to the collapsing Third Reich, with its attendant violence and self-destruction.

All five chapters ahead recount and assess the complex relationships Germans had with the National Socialist state – and with one another – within shifting contexts for action from 1933 to 1945. It is important to note that within these shifting contexts, there was room for realignment of persons and groups across the five categories of social experience. The reality of Germans' lives under Hitler was complex and dynamic. No category of analysis is hard and fast. Significant class, regional and religious differences remained in the Third Reich, so that Germans can be identified, according to context, in more than one way. Nor do the categories used here deny change over time. As we shall see, some enthusiasts later became disenchanted and some accomplices became resisters, even as some who initially dissented came to back the regime. There were also cases of multiple realignments. To respect such complexity, this book considers the lives and responses of a wide cross-section of Germans and qualifies its generalizations as appropriate.

CHAPTER 1
BEGINNINGS (1933–1935)

The Third Reich began in flames. On 30 January 1933, the day Adolf Hitler became Chancellor of Germany, a fiery river flowed through the central avenues of Berlin. Men in brown and black uniforms marched under the Brandenburg Gate with blazing torches held aloft in celebration. Torchlight parades took place in other cities over the following week, with bonfires set in smaller villages. Just a few weeks later, on the morning of 28 February, smoke billowed from Berlin's federal parliament building, the *Reichstag*. Hitler immediately exploited the arson attack, most likely committed by an angry Dutch anarchist, with the Decree for the Protection of the People and State (Reichstag Fire Decree). Valid until further notice, it suspended all civil rights and legalized a programme of unrestrained terror against the Nazis' political opponents. The first prisoners entered the gates of Dachau concentration camp the next month.

On 5 March 1933, Germans went to the polls once again. The Nazi Party gained 44 per cent of the vote, but by forming a majority coalition with his conservative partners and with the support of the parties of the middle, Hitler easily passed the Law to Remedy the Distress of People and State (Enabling Act) on 23 March. It legally transformed Germany into a dictatorship by giving Hitler unlimited authority to override the Weimar constitution throughout Germany's seventeen states. A boycott of Jewish businesses in April and demolition of labour unions in May signalled the regime's commitment to comprehensive 'coordination' (*Gleichschaltung*) of German public life, synchronizing it with Nazi passions and prejudices at every level. By July 1933, all political parties other than the NSDAP were illegal.

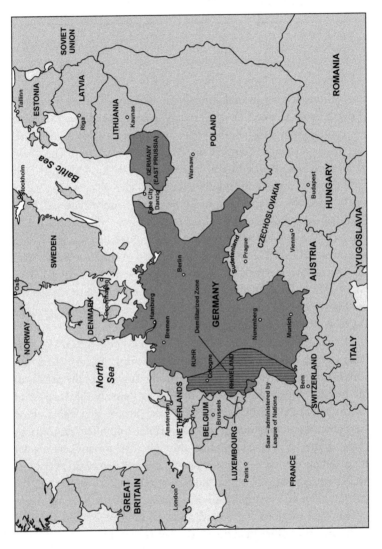

Map 1. Germany in 1933.

Figure 1.1 A torchlight parade in Berlin celebrates Hitler's Chancellorship, 30 January 1933 (Bundesarchiv, Bild 102-02985A/Georg Pahl).

Coordination (*Gleichschaltung*)

With the Enabling Act (23 March 1933), the Nazi regime began the thorough coordination (i.e. synchronization or nazification) of German society in line with Hitler's vision for this. The first objective was to consolidate political power with the creation of an authoritarian, one-party Reich. A mass of legislation secured it by eliminating the independence of individual state, regional and municipal governments. Yet *Gleichschaltung* meant more than establishing a system of control. Its policies aimed to infuse all of Germany's old political, social and cultural institutions with Nazi values in order to serve new Nazi goals.

Thereafter a series of measures formalized legal persecution of outsiders. These ranged from the Law for the Prevention of

Hereditarily Diseased Offspring (14 July 1933), which mandated compulsory sterilization for Germans with physical and intellectual disabilities, to the Nuremberg Laws (15 September 1935), which forbade marriage or intimate relationships between 'Aryan' Germans and 'non-Aryans', and demoted the latter from citizens to subjects of the state. This period witnessed waves of antisemitic violence, peaking in 1933 and again in 1935.

Germany also took its first steps towards dismantling the hated Treaty of Versailles. After leaving the League of Nations in October 1933, Hitler oversaw clandestine expansion of the armed forces; in March 1935, he reintroduced military conscription in open violation of the Treaty. The priority he gave to the armed forces (*Wehrmacht*) required coordinating the Nazis' own paramilitary organization, the SA, as well. Between 30 June and 2 July 1934, Hitler launched what became known as the Night of the Long Knives, when SS squads and armed forces units murdered scores of Stormtroopers, including their Chief, Ernst Röhm. In taming all elements of dissent within his movement and eliminating any significant political resistance from without, Hitler was well positioned to assume supreme power when President Hindenburg died on 2 August 1934. He abolished the office of President and made himself *Führer* of the German People and Reich Chancellor. By 1935, the Nazi dictatorship was firmly established.

Nazis

The system of rule in Nazi Germany centred on one charismatic personality, Hitler himself. Race, expansion, violence and dictatorship formed the core of his world view, which he had articulated in his political manifesto, *My Struggle* (*Mein Kampf*). His National Socialist devotees, who saw the *Führer* as an almost supernaturally gifted being, shared these core ideas. In their view, strong 'Aryans' and weak, parasitic – yet still dangerous – Jews were engaged in an eternal Social Darwinist struggle. Only a strong man like Hitler, they believed, could achieve living space in the East, eliminate the Jewish threat and save the German race.

The unique, highly authoritarian *Führer* state took some time to emerge, but after Hindenburg's death, it became fully operational. At the top was Adolf Hitler, head of both the Nazi Party and the German state. Below him, on one hand, were the Reich Leaders, responsible for special tasks within the Party, and heading its divisions, affiliations and sponsored organizations. On the other, there were federal government ministers and newly appointed Reich Governors, who oversaw the administration of Germany's formerly self-governing states, such as Baden, Bavaria and Saxony. In many cases, 'old fighters' (long-time NSDAP members) gained both Party and state positions. Many figures could be mentioned, but only the most important Nazi leaders appear here. Who those were shifted somewhat over time. In 1933–5, three men were especially significant: Hermann Goering, Minister-President of Prussia and head of its secret state police (the *Gestapo*); Heinrich Himmler, head of the SS; and Joseph Goebbels, Minister of Propaganda and People's Enlightenment. As they carved out their personal fiefdoms, they competed with, and duplicated the responsibilities of, other Party and state officials. For this reason, the Third Reich has sometimes been called a polycracy, a state with overlapping authorities and multiple power centres under Hitler's supreme authority. The system of 'multilevel governance' seemed chaotic at times, but it proved enormously adaptable, which helped the Nazi regime remain in power.[1]

Hitler rarely gave clear instructions to his underlings, especially in writing, and from 1934, he grew increasingly distant from everyday decision-making, particularly in domestic policy. This hardly made him a 'weak dictator'.[2] Hitler set the overarching goals and sometimes offered guidelines; those below had to meet them as best they could. Thus, his style of rule empowered others to 'work towards the *Führer*', to direct their activities in the service of his will as they interpreted it.[3] In turn, competition for Hitler's favour encouraged ever more extreme solutions to the problems he identified, resulting in what is often described as the 'cumulative radicalization' of the Nazi regime. Neither Hitler's intentions alone, nor those of his followers, explain how things happened; forces from below engaged with his ambitions from above to shape decisions, processes and outcomes.

Coming to power ironically triggered an identity crisis for the Nazi Party. Without rival parties, what was the NSDAP's new reason for being? According to Hitler, it was to provide leadership of the *Volk*, not only through schooling Germans in the key ideological tenets of Nazism but also by watching over them. The Party's upper-level political leaders, however, now gained roles that went beyond education and surveillance. The majority of the thirty or so Regional Leaders (*Gauleiter*) of the NSDAP's main territorial divisions enjoyed enhanced prestige and salaries from their inroads into administration, once the preserve of the federal states. Most gained some formal government office by the end of 1933, some as Reich Governors. Others assumed various state responsibilities unofficially. Some of the approximately 800 NSDAP District Leaders (*Kreisleiter*) merged Party and local governmental positions as well, by becoming county councillors and mayors. In the absence of jurisdictional clarity about their roles, these Nazi functionaries came into significant conflict with established state authorities, much to their frustration. Yet Hitler had never intended a total absorption of the state by the Nazi Party at any level. He recognized Party members' lack of administrative expertise and aimed to minimize disruption.

That original office-holders therefore often remained – if they were 'Aryan' and politically reliable – keenly disappointed lower-ranking 'old fighters' who felt let down, despite the heady euphoria of Hitler's first months in power. They were especially disgusted by the hundreds of thousands of Germans who now jumped on the bandwagon and joined the Nazi Party. Unlike these opportunistic 'March violets' – so named because they joined after the Nazis' strong showing in the March 1933 election – 'old fighters' had suffered for the cause in the Weimar Republic. Their long-time Party membership and service did not always pay dividends. Many things remained 'the same as before', complained one Nazi bank clerk in 1934.[4] Few gained municipal office and they watched recent, often better educated, joiners gain positions in the Party bureaucracy. Worse, many 'old fighters' remained unemployed. Approximately 300,000 early members left the Party by 1935, some embittered by unfulfilled expectations for personal gain, others feeling betrayed in the wake of the Night of the Long Knives.[5]

Most stayed on, believing that the promised privileges of membership in the *Volksgemeinschaft* would eventually compensate for personal disappointments.

Long-standing female Nazi Party members also had complaints. Some had believed in a special, independent role for women once Hitler was in power, despite the Nazi movement's decidedly antifeminist, misogynistic nature. Those women were soon sidelined, then ousted. Within one year, no woman leader from the Weimar days remained in any major Nazi Party office. Younger, more subservient women replaced them all, in roles that remained largely honorary. Gertrud Scholtz-Klink, the new head of the National Socialist Women's Organization in 1934, is a prime example. As Reich Women's Leader, she had a grand title but little real authority.

By contrast, Reich Leader SS Heinrich Himmler saw his power significantly enhanced. The SS originated in the mid-1920s as a bodyguard to protect Hitler and other prominent Party figures, but Himmler had more ambitious plans: the SS was to become the elite racial vanguard of the *Volksgemeinschaft*. He now aimed to improve the quality of his SS men, numbering approximately 50,000 in January 1933. Most were military veterans, Nazi Party 'old fighters' and unemployed university students, but his recruitment efforts soon attracted PhD holders, aristocrats and even some military officers among the nearly 150,000 men who joined in the months thereafter. Cautious about the ideological commitment of these new applicants, Himmler closed off entry to the SS in April and then threatened to reduce their number. He later boasted of having expelled 60,000 SS men in these years: alcoholics, homosexuals, those lacking documented generations of pure 'Aryan' ancestry and those he deemed insufficiently fanatical. However, resentment from long-time SS members, who served without pay, prevented such a thorough cleansing from ever taking place.[6]

By 1934, Himmler became chief of the political police forces – tasked with rooting out political opposition – in all states except Prussia where Goering was in charge. A power struggle ensued, but in appointing Himmler as Inspector of Prussia's *Gestapo* that year, Goering conceded defeat. The SS took over the *Gestapo*, transformed existing political police forces across the country into secret ones, and coordinated them with a central *Gestapo* office in Berlin. Reinhard Heydrich (already Chief of the SS Security Service, the SS intelligence agency) became its head. SS men gained additional top positions within the *Gestapo* and other police forces as well, and increasingly replaced the Stormtroopers as concentration camp guards. Himmler and the SS demonstrated their utmost loyalty to Hitler during the Night of the Long Knives, ensuring their dominant standing going forward.

Until those events of June 1934, the numerically dominant Brownshirts enjoyed their heyday. The SA had been the paramilitary arm of the NSDAP since 1922. Its members were predominantly working-class and lower-middle-class men who were deeply antisemitic and virulently opposed to communism. With Hitler as Chancellor, SA membership swelled. From 430,000 men in 1932, it grew to four million by April 1934.[7] Those men now had the state-sanctioned privilege to exact revenge on their political enemies and assault their racial ones. Thousands of German communists, socialists and Jews suffered at their hands. Vicious beatings often resulted in death or permanent injury. Personal enrichment – stealing and looting from their victims – was another SA perquisite. The SA had a prominent, highly visible role in the mass spectacles of these early years too: they marched with flaming torches, stood as sentries outside stores during boycotts, set so-called un-German literature alight in city squares and bellowed their approval of Hitler at the Nazi Party Rallies, which drew together Party formations from across Germany each year in Nuremberg.

What long-time Stormtroopers expected most from the new regime, however, was a job. Despite some government efforts to provide them with one, and despite state money now flowing to SA coffers, many individual Brownshirts remained unemployed; their social status did not improve. Worse, they now had to compete with better-educated new Nazis. As spring turned to summer in 1934, and Hitler's most revolutionary promises remained unfulfilled, unrest festered. Half of the men who belonged to the SA in 1931 had left by early 1934, even as overall numbers swelled. Among those who remained, calls for a second revolution grew louder. From the regime's perspective,

Figure 1.2 SA men prepare for the boycott against stores and businesses owned by Jewish Germans in Munich on 1 April 1933 (bpk Bildagentur/ Heinrich Hoffmann /Art Resource, New York).

continued SA violence and revolutionary talk threatened stability at home, damaged the image of the regime abroad and endangered the Nazis' alliance with the German military. SA Chief Ernst Röhm was a rival to the *Führer* himself. Although there were never any real plans for a Röhm-led *putsch*, Hitler – supported by Himmler's SS – launched the purge that tamed his former revolutionary vanguard; it also served as a pretext for settling scores with conservative leaders who had crossed him.

The Night of the Long Knives officially took at least ninety-one lives, most of them SA men. Hundreds of thousands of Stormtroopers were also summarily dismissed. Humiliation lingered, especially since Hitler justified the murders by referencing homosexuality in the SA, which needed to be eliminated. Yet this was by no means the end of the SA's story in the Third Reich. It remained one of the Nazi Party's biggest mass organizations under a new chief, Victor Lutze.

Stormtroopers were particularly instrumental in spreading antisemitic propaganda and initiating anti-Jewish violence in the months before the September 1935 Nuremberg Laws.

If excitement about the future of Nazism had dimmed among some old Nazis, it surged among the young ones after 1933. By the end of the year, approximately 1.7 million German boys aged ten to eighteen belonged to the Hitler Youth (HJ); 600,000 girls belonged to the equivalent female branch, the League of German Girls (BDM).[8] Baldur von Schirach, who became head of the organization in 1933, shared Hitler's desire to integrate all 'Aryan' young people within it. Other parties' youth leagues were dissolved and even right-leaning groups were forcibly coordinated. Children and youth signed up out of genuine ideological commitment to the Nazi cause, simple curiosity, parental opportunism or, as one former HJ member recalled, to ensure they were not 'left out in the cold'.[9] By 1935, membership was still voluntary, but it continued to grow.

The HJ and BDM worked on German youngsters to fill them with love for the *Führer*, the Fatherland and their racial equals, and with hatred for political, social and racial enemies. At the same time, these organizations offered pleasurable activities like hiking, marching, war games, folk songs and campfires. Girls especially relished new freedoms from family and school, and challenging gender norms despite constant sermons on the value of motherhood. 'What I liked', recounted one former BDM girl, 'was that you were allowed to do lots of [forbidden] stuff … . Like marching, climbing trees, stuff like that.'[10] Others enjoyed the *Volksgemeinschaft* in miniature as working-class and middle-class Germans mixed, often for the first time. Those ideological messages were affirmed in public school classrooms, where Germany's 300,000 teachers – one-third of whom joined the Nazi Party – followed a regime-approved curriculum.[11] Young Germans played active parts in the key events of 1933–5. HJ boys stood alongside Stormtroopers to prevent shopping at Jewish-owned stores during the April boycott. BDM girls distributed antisemitic propaganda. Children jeered at 'racial defilers' (violators of the Nuremberg Laws) paraded through town, singing songs about Jews' blood spurting from knives.

Figure 1.3 Hitler Youth and League of German Girls members march together in 1934 (Ullstein Bild via Getty Images/Hans Henschke).

Whether these actions equated to a wholehearted, inner alignment with National Socialist ideology is difficult to assess. With their range of motives for participating in these organizations, we might hesitate to call children who enjoyed HJ and BDM outings and events 'Nazis', but we can be less reticent in so labelling older youth at universities. Many had belonged to the National Socialist German Students' League before 1933. Nazi students led the collection and public burning of so-called un-German books in May that year and provided an important surveillance mechanism to ensure professors' and administrators' compliance with Nazi ideas. Few of their number expressed disappointment with the Third Reich. The economy was recovering, employment opportunities were opening up and university graduates had new career paths. Overall, post-secondary students were among the most consistently enthusiastic groups of Nazis between 1933 and 1935.

Significantly, then, it was sometimes the long-term fanatics – the oldest fighters – whom Nazi Germany disappointed most deeply after 1933. Their expectations had been the highest. The majority nonetheless maintained their loyalty to their *Führer*, while complaining energetically about his underlings. The regime's later achievements also provided compensation for ongoing frustrations and reinvigorated their fervour.

Accomplices

Conservative politicians and members of the traditional elites welcomed the new government in 1933 nearly as warmly as the Nazis. Despite some reservations, these Germans were willing, even eager, to work with it. Such men included high-ranking civil servants, judges, leading industrialists, large landowners, university professors and senior military officers. Many were upper-class, wealthy and of aristocratic backgrounds. They shared qualms about Hitler's plebeian origins, the brutal, thuggish activities of the SA and the vulgar slogans of Nazi propaganda. They expressed even greater concern about the socialist (i.e. anti-capitalist) elements of National Socialism. Very few conservative elites had joined the Nazi Party before 1933. Nonetheless, they concluded that Hitler was better than the Weimar Republic. Democracy had threatened their once dominant position in German politics and society. They wanted it secured and saw Hitler as a means to achieve this. If they did not greet the dawn of the Third Reich with 'Heil Hitler', then they at least met it with 'open arms'.[12]

Germany's elite circles were optimistic about the new coalition government in January 1933 for two reasons. First, they believed their allies in cabinet were mapping the route, while President Paul von Hindenburg, a fellow conservative, remained in the driver's seat. It was Hitler, they believed, who was along for the ride. With only three Nazis in cabinet, the conservative majority was sure it could control a politically naïve Hitler and constrain Nazi extremism. 'We've hired him', Vice Chancellor Franz von Papen boasted.[13] Second, they recognized considerable overlap in interests with the Nazis. They shared both hatreds and desires: targets to destroy (democracy, communism, socialism, labour unions, the Treaty of Versailles, 'degenerate' culture and Jewish influence in society and the economy) and things to build (authoritarian government, military strength and restored national pride). These men also generally supported Hitler's immediate strategies to reach these goals, including new elections, suspending the constitution and establishing a dictatorial regime. The Third Reich could never have happened without their initial and ongoing support.

The conservative politicians seemed oblivious to how much they were loathed and distrusted by the Nazis, who viewed them as entitled, timid old gentlemen, reactionary rather than revolutionary like themselves. Still, since their collaboration was vital for demolishing the Weimar Republic, Hitler camouflaged his anti-conservatism at the outset. His play-acting was especially effective at the Day of Potsdam on 21 March 1933, an elaborate celebration to mark the new government. This ritual of reassurance was meant to convince Hindenburg of his undiminished authority and Hitler's desire to cooperate with his coalition partners. In the most famous photograph from that day, amid fluttering Imperial black, white and red flags, a deferential Hitler, in civilian dress, bows to Hindenburg. Lesser-known ones show conservative cabinet members beside Hitler acknowledging cheers from the crowd. They assumed they had achieved a fusion of traditional German conservatism with dynamic, populist Nazism.

Because they believed it would deal the fatal blow to socialism and communism, conservative politicians supported the Enabling Act on 23 March, which gave Hitler and his cabinet unrestrained powers – for the next four years – to enact laws and alter the Weimar constitution. Hitler's Brownshirt uniform and the massive swastika flag, combined

Figure 1.4 The new Chancellor and his cabinet members, conservatives and Nazis, on the Day of Potsdam (23 March 1933). Vice Chancellor Franz von Papen is on Hitler's immediate right (Ullstein Bild via Getty Images/Robert Sennecke).

with the forcible exclusion of Communist deputies from the *Reichstag*, sent a clear message that day: the Nazis were now in charge of government. 'Old fighters' gained new cabinet posts created by Hitler. Nazi thugs intimidated and even physically assaulted conservative politicians. On 27 June 1933, the German National People's Party dissolved itself just before the official decree forbidding any party but the NSDAP. Its head announced his resignation from cabinet two days later.

Despite the sidelining, and then silencing, of conservative politicians, traditional elites, especially top civil servants, still believed they could influence Hitler. Indeed, Hitler's own actions were constrained in this period by not wanting to alienate influential men like career diplomat and Foreign Minister Konstantin von Neurath and Justice Minister Franz Gürtner, who already held these positions before 1933. Personnel continuities reassured senior bureaucrats, who were relieved to see the same faces, whether it was in the diplomatic corps, the military leadership or in German courtrooms, where the vast majority remained in their positions. Continuities in pre-1933 agendas also comforted the traditional elites. This was especially true for foreign policy, which at first seemed familiar and in line with established approaches to revising the post-Great War order. Germany's departure from the League of Nations was welcome to the conservatives, as were Hitler's speeches demanding alterations to the Treaty of Versailles, particularly the provisions restricting the armed forces; they cheered the introduction of conscription in 1935. Here nationalist, authoritarian and aggressively revisionist agendas overlapped.

The Nazis secured the traditional elites' consent with a seductive blend of continuity and change, apparent restoration alongside radical revisions. German judges are a case in point. They loudly applauded both what they saw as a 'return' to law and order and relished new, unprecedented powers to interpret it. The appearance of a normally functioning legal system was critical to legitimizing Nazi power. From 1933 to 1945, a traditional judicial apparatus – one that managed trials, convicted defendants, listened to appeals and sent Germans to 'regular' prisons and penitentiaries – not only coexisted, but also intersected, with the novel elements of the Nazi state, which inflicted extralegal brutality on its enemies. Justice Minister Gürtner personified the judges' positive attitude to the new regime. He certainly shared its authoritarian sympathies, being unrelentingly opposed to liberal democracy. Gürtner never questioned Hitler's authority to make law nor challenged Nazi ideas as the basis for legal decisions. He, like most German judges, accepted that the '*Volk*'s healthy instinct' should guide their sentencing. If in doubt, they simply needed to ask themselves: What would Hitler do?[14] Gürtner readily approved laws like the 1933 Reichstag Fire Decree, which served as a kind of constitution for Nazi Germany. No breaches of traditional legal principles, such as granting the police unlimited powers, seemed too extreme to eradicate communism. Even judges less ardently committed to the Third Reich complied because they believed in the rule of law. The most shocking violations, they managed to convince themselves, were only temporary measures that protected against future unlawfulness.

Personal gains and privileges also dispelled initial misgivings and guaranteed elite support. In April 1933, the Law for the Restoration of the Professional Civil Service dismissed thousands of 'non-Aryan' (i.e. Jewish) and politically suspect Germans from state employment, including university professors. Most expelled academics fled abroad. Among them were twenty-four past and future Nobel Prize winners, most famously Albert Einstein, the brilliant physicist. Their former colleagues at German universities, technical schools and research institutes gained new opportunities for career advancement. Hitler certainly did not need university professors to stay in power. Possessing only an eighth-grade education, he was profoundly hostile to intellectualism and especially scornful of the ivory tower, which exalted academic freedom over obedience. Yet a 'yes' from these influential intellectual elites would ease Germany's transition from democracy to dictatorship. Most adapted effortlessly to the new order, and for reasons beyond mere opportunism. German academics were, for the most part, deeply nationalist, anti-liberal, intensely anti-communist and frequently antisemitic. Few had voted for the Nazi Party before 1933, but some now embraced Nazism very energetically. The well-known philosopher Martin Heidegger, Rector of Freiburg University, for example, joined the Party in 1933. Accommodation among academics also proceeded smoothly because there was no central control over research and scholarship under the swastika. Intellectual positions hostile to the Nazi world view were naturally unacceptable, and the only path to career success lay in unambiguous outward loyalty to the regime, but ideological inroads varied with the discipline. In many fields, much was allowed to remain the same, in classroom lectures as with individual research projects.

Nazi Germany offered new routes of upward mobility within the legal profession with Jewish Germans purged and careers to be made in the field of anti-Jewish law. Judges could also preside over new Nazi courts established for specific crimes. Nazi Party membership was not required: only half of German judges ever joined. These included

Figure 1.5 German judges swear an oath of allegiance to Hitler and Germany in the State Opera House in Berlin, 1933 (Corbis via Getty Images/Hulton-Deutsch).

Special Courts and People's Courts. The former dealt with violators of new 'treachery laws', which prohibited slander against the regime; the latter heard high treason and treason charges against those who actively resisted the state. The new Hereditary Health Courts, where judges sentenced disabled and 'asocial' Germans to mandatory sterilization, offered additional prospects for career progress.

The Nazi assumption of power brought some gains for the land-owning aristocracy too. Though they had steadfastly opposed the 'Marxist' Republic, which seemed to deprioritize agricultural issues, the populist elements of National Socialism worried them. Their concerns grew when devout Nazi Richard Walther Darré became the new Minister of Agriculture in June 1933. His 'blood and soil' ideals, praising landholding peasants as the font of a pure German race and true German culture, were hostile to hereditary noblemen like themselves. Darré even promised to return land 'stolen' by the aristocracy to the peasantry. That threat never materialized. Eager to address the propertied elite's concerns, the Nazi state followed policies that ultimately secured their future on their land and benefitted them disproportionately. These included the 1933 Hereditary Farm Law (which prevented banks from repossessing farms in debt), Eastern Aid subsidies (which provided financial support for bankrupt estates) and high tariffs on imported food products. Moreover, in the spirit of compromise that marked this early period, the regime allowed estate owners some autonomy in agrarian matters. As we shall see, landed elites shared peasant farmers' complaints about the regime. Yet big agriculture was healthier after 1933 than it had been in years. Big business could soon say the same.

Industrial elites did not bring the Nazis to power, as their left-wing opponents claimed, but they were complicit in consolidating that power and, critically, laying the foundations for war. The relationship between the Nazi regime and the heads of the largest German companies, like Krupp, Degussa and BASF, was complex and contradictory. On the one hand, major captains of industry viewed the Nazi Party's virulent anti-communism with pleasure, to be exploited to end union demands and labour unrest. On the other, business leaders were suspicious of the Nazis' anti-capitalist rhetoric, not to mention its working-class supporters. They also worried about Nazi radicalism's effect on economic recovery from the Great Depression. Few of these men were true friends of democracy. They therefore approached the new government with 'goodwill, but not too much enthusiasm', as one industrial titan put it.[15] Yet by spring 1933, roughly one third of the board members of the largest industrial firms in Germany had joined the Nazi Party.[16] Business leaders generally found Hitler to be less threatening to economic stability than they had feared. Hjalmar Schacht's appointment as Economics Minister in 1934 was especially heartening. This long-serving President of the German Central Bank saw Hitler as the only remedy for the Great Depression, but naïvely believed economic interests would be prioritized over Nazi ideological goals.

Gustav Krupp's path illustrates the adaptability of big business elites. The head of one of Germany's leading industrial and munition-making companies had originally expressed reservations about

Hitler; once in power, the Nazi regime had his full support. Krupp assisted in designing, implementing and gaining acceptance for new policies affecting industry, above all those focused on rearmament. By 1934, the Nazi government was already spending three times as much on military projects as civilian ones. Industrial leaders approved of rearmament as a spur to general economic recovery, even as they grumbled about the methods for achieving it. They criticized, for example, the 1934 New Plan, which imposed restrictions on importing raw materials in line with the regime's drive for autarky (economic self-sufficiency). Companies needed those materials to fill rearmament contracts. At the same time, they collaborated closely with the regime in schemes for financing rearmament.

German industrialists also welcomed Nazi moves to curb labour unrest. These included the dissolution of the trade unions from 2 May 1933, the outlawing of collective bargaining and the promise by Robert Ley, head of the newly established German Labour Front (DAF) – the sole labour organization in Nazi Germany – to restore absolute authority to the rightful leader of a factory (the employer). Even those decisions not in the industrialists' hands, such as state-directed wage freezes, cuts and controls, usually worked in their favour. These allowed some companies to hire more employees but pay them less, satisfying the regime's need for job creation while contributing to the owners' profits.

German Labour Front (DAF)

The German Labour Front was the labour organization that replaced Germany's various trade unions after they were outlawed on 2 May 1933, their assets seized and many of their leaders arrested. It did not aim to represent workers alone; employers and members of the professions, like doctors and lawyers, were also meant to join. In theory, the DAF was created to allow workers and employers to represent their mutual interests. In reality, the Labour Front was the heavy-handed arm of the Nazi Party within the working world. DAF membership was supposedly voluntary, but getting a job in most branches of German commerce or industry was very difficult without it.

It was clearly not always business as usual. The Nazi state forced companies into prioritizing different products necessary for rearmament, and new regulations affected prices and foreign trading. But in this period, most major firms and their directors had some 'room for manoeuvre' so long as the Nazis' goals – which they usually shared – were met.[17] By 1935, it was apparent that the Nazis were good for business: militarizing the economy was instrumental in leading Germany out of the Depression. Industrialists also profited from unofficial, ad-hoc 'Aryanization' (the transfer of Jewish-owned property to non-Jews). By 1935, 'Aryans' had acquired up to 25 per cent of Jewish businesses, usually at heavily discounted prices. For some firms, like the Degussa metals and chemical company and the Flick steel and coal conglomerate, buying up Jewish concerns led to wider profit margins even in these early years. Yet there was more to business elites' embrace of the Third Reich than the drive for profits. As German patriots, they were genuinely inspired by the promise of national renewal.

The Nazis' accomplices in the officer corps of the armed forces reaped different rewards. In January 1933, this group had the most leverage among the traditional elites, since Hitler absolutely needed them on side. They had once sworn an oath to the Weimar constitution, but most were vehemently anti-republican and even more deeply opposed to communism and socialism, despite a claim to be above politics. As did all conservatives, they wanted order at home – an end to Weimar's perpetual political and social unrest – and revisions to the Treaty of Versailles. Like General Werner von Blomberg, Minister of Defence in Hitler's first cabinet, most believed Hitler would achieve both, viewing the new government as 'the first glimpse of light since 1918'.[18] For the next three years, Hitler took careful steps to cement his alliance with the military.

Military elites were privy to, and supportive of, his long-term aggressive intentions. On 3 February 1933, he outlined plans to his top commanders for 'Germanizing' conquered land in the East by expelling all native inhabitants. In the same speech, he also promised to exterminate socialism and communism. In February 1935, the newly announced *Luftwaffe* (Air Force) gained a mandate to expand under Goering's command. In March 1935, conscription quintupled the number of soldiers and provided new opportunities for promotion in the re-christened *Wehrmacht*. Hitler brought the German navy on board via the 1935 Anglo-German Naval Agreement, which gave the green light to growing and modernizing Germany's fleet. These actions deepened the commitment of military officers to the Nazi state. Although the majority of officers were never Party members, they were certainly in line with Nazism, and from 2 August 1934, at the armed forces' own initiative (not a *Führer* order), all existing military personnel and thousands of future recruits pledged personal loyalty – until the death – to Adolf Hitler himself. As they saw it, their position of power had been restored; with it, Germany would return to its rightful place internationally. In short, Germany's military leaders were big winners in the Third Reich's first three years.

The German elites' world view extended beyond approving anti-Versailles foreign policy, rearmament and increased 'law and order'. It also overlapped with key tenets of Nazi ideology. The Nazis did not invent the idea of a racially based *Volksgemeinschaft*. Some nationalist thinkers had long promoted the vision of a community defined by blood, not class, region or religion, which brought the right Germans inside but kept 'un-Germans' out. The prototypical 'un-German' for most elites was the Jew. Since the turn of the century, the Jews symbolized 'the multiple ills of modernity' undermining the old traditions and customs.[19] Landed estate owners blamed Jews for urbanization and the resulting flight from the land. Industrialists feared that Jews empowered workers. Most condemned their supposed role in the decline of Christianity and traditional morality, and denounced their connections to socialism and communism. Elite antisemitism was not identical to Nazi racist thinking about the Jews, but it was pervasive, and many, as we have already seen, stood to benefit directly from the regime's anti-Jewish policies. At times, they outpaced the Nazis themselves. Judges rushed to extend the 1935 Nuremberg Laws' implications, criminalizing ever more interactions between insider and outsider Germans. Though the 'Aryan Paragraph' (part of the 1933 Civil Service Law) did not initially apply to the armed forces, Defence Minister von Blomberg voluntarily put it into effect in early 1934. The military too, he said, should be a 'community of blood'.[20]

While they supported discriminatory action in principle, conservative elites did complain about specific, anti-Jewish measures being excessively violent, improvised or random. Compassion for their fellow Germans did not move them. Concerns about the effects on international opinion, domestic stability and economic recovery did. Foreign Minister von Neurath feared disapproval abroad over the regime-ordered boycott of Jewish stores and businesses in 1933; Finance Minister Schacht supported the 1935 Nuremberg Laws because he hoped they would end the brutal, uncontrolled actions that preceded them; land-owning aristocrats refused to stop dealing with Jewish cattle traders, because it was still profitable. Unlike the Nazis, for whom all Jews were 'un-German', conservative elites sometimes sought exemptions on a case-by-case basis. This Jew could be included in Germany's future, they said, but Jews as a group could not. Almost none said anything different.

Similarly, there was little disagreement with the Nazis' eugenic programmes, which targeted 'diseased' and 'asocial' Germans. Medical faculty in university clinics readily performed sterilizations ordered by judges in Hereditary Health Courts, despite some uneasiness among Catholic elites about the practice. The regime's persecution of homosexuals had almost total support here. From 1935, legal theorists drafted amendments to the penal code mandating increasingly draconian punishments for homosexual behaviour. Judges complied, sending more gay men to regular prisons or penitentiaries than the *Gestapo* sent to concentration camps.

Coercion and intimidation played a role, though a subordinate one, in ensuring elite cooperation. The Nazis threatened business leaders who challenged coordination, for example, with strong-arm tactics like search and arrests, allegations of tax evasion and forced managerial replacements. Judges who witnessed the effects of Nazi violence on defendants in their courtrooms were less likely to step out of line. The Night of the Long Knives in June 1934 terrified some within the elite ranks into conformity – several of their number were among the victims – but the murders solidified the support of others by repressing unruly, activist National Socialists. German military elites welcomed the firm subordination of a competing institution. Well-educated, frequently financially secure and relatively powerful, this group overall had less to fear and more leeway for personal choice of action than did most Germans under Nazi rule between 1933 and 1935. Time and again, they chose to support the new Germany.

After the Night of the Long Knives, President von Hindenburg expressed his personal gratitude to Hitler for saving the German people from a serious danger. Like many elites, he believed Hitler had made Germany safe from democracy itself. When this supreme icon of the old, pre-Weimar order died on 2 August 1934, any remaining hope of controlling Hitler evaporated. Still, conservative elites continued to applaud foreign policy successes, profit-raising rearmament drives and the eradication of the leftist threat. Exemptions and exceptions soothed anxieties about extreme violence towards Jewish Germans. Yet by helping to birth and nurture the Third Reich, Hitler's accomplices unwittingly guaranteed the destruction of what they had hoped to restore.

Supporters

The support of the majority German population was also crucial for maintaining Hitler's hold on power. They were not communists or socialists (or had seen the error of their ways if they once were). They were not Jewish or otherwise racially 'alien'. They did not engage in 'asocial' behaviours, commit homosexual 'crimes' or write 'un-German' books. Most of them never joined the NSDAP, the SA or the SS. Nonetheless, within this group there was genuine widespread adoration of the *Führer*, acclaim for his accomplishments and some commitment to Nazism's central ideological tenets. For those not yet converted to the Nazi faith, coercion ensured compliance. For example, treachery laws led to *Gestapo* arrests for a wealth of violations (spreading rumours, telling jokes about important Nazis, singing forbidden songs and more). 'Racial defilement' – violating the Nuremberg Laws – could lead to public shaming and incarceration. Without minimizing Nazi Germany's brutality, it is important to acknowledge that only a small minority of insiders, and an even smaller one before the war, ever saw the insides of police interrogation rooms, prison cells and concentration camps. The limits to fear and the role of Nazi terror must therefore be recognized as much as their extent. Ultimately, whether 'ordinary' insiders did so out of conviction, ambivalence or fear, they generally cooperated with the Nazis, or at least managed to adjust. By coming inside the Third Reich, they normalized it, including its worst abuses.

One response to Hitler's new government was to join the Nazi Party. Its membership stood at approximately 900,000 in January

Figure 1.6 Germans cheer Hitler's assumption of the dual role as *Führer* of the German People and Reich Chancellor, August 1934 (FPG/Hulton Archive/Getty Images).

1933; by April, it had grown by 1.6 million.[21] It is impossible to determine Germans' innermost reasons for becoming card-carrying Party members or indeed members of any of its divisions or affiliated organizations. Affinity, opportunism and coercion all played their part. So did the fact that everybody seemed to be doing it. Indeed, the feeling of being excluded was unbearable to many. Upon joining the German Labour Front in October 1933, one young woman who had formerly sympathized with anti-Nazi parties wrote in her diary, 'All this being on the sidelines ... [to] end up an outsider ... that's not what I want.'[22] *Not* joining the Party certainly did not signal opposition to the regime. The cost of dues, the time commitment of duties and meetings, and extra attention from authorities could be off-putting. In general, membership was not mandatory.

The cooperation of German workers was critical, as they represented the greatest potential threat to the stability of the Third Reich. The proletariat (working class) – Germany's largest social class – had voted overwhelmingly for the communist and socialist parties before 1933, although some estimates indicate almost one in four cast ballots for the Nazi Party at the end of the Weimar Republic. As swastika flags appeared in working-class neighbourhoods in the wake of police violence and Nazi terror directed against suspected opponents, residents wondered if they were an attempt to ward off future harassment or a symbol of authentic conversion to Nazism. Both were possibilities.

The working-class experience in the final Weimar years had been stamped by record unemployment. Recognizing its devastating socio-economic impact, the Nazi regime immediately committed to conquering unemployment with work-creation schemes. The Reinhardt Plan, introduced in June 1933, made more than one billion *Reichsmarks* available for public works projects: construction, water works, road building (including the well-known '*Führer*'s highways', the *Autobahn*) – bridge repair and general maintenance. The number of job seekers began to decline significantly. Official statistics told an even better story by omitting 'non-Aryans' dismissed by the Civil Service Law. While it was to be several years before the majority of workers had more money in their pockets – employment remained well below pre-1929 levels from 1933 to 1935 – the return to work in any form, to some kind of normality after Weimar's crisis years, certainly made adapting to the Third Reich easier.

Work-creation schemes declined as rearmament accelerated. Now there were jobs building military facilities, like barracks, airfields and fortifications. Munitions companies slowly started hiring additional employees. With trade unions banned and a centralized German Labour Front, a new system of industrial relations emerged on the factory floor. Strikes, though not technically illegal, occurred far less often and were ended quickly. Low, controlled wages meant extra income came only through longer overtime hours. Pressure to join the Labour Front meant paying membership dues. Employers reported poor worker discipline: increasing absenteeism, intentional work slowdowns, minor sabotage and low turnout at official meetings. There is certainly evidence for characterizing the German workers' mood in this period as 'depressed and critical'.[23] Yet on-the-ground intelligence varied. Secret reports sent to SOPADE, the Social Democratic Party in Exile in Prague, acknowledged 'widespread toleration of Nazism', at least among workers in heavy industry in some locations.[24]

Fear naturally played a role in forcing outward conformity. Surveillance was extensive and there could be frightening consequences for stepping out of line. Yet workers' 'toleration' of Nazism should not generally be understood as a mere ploy to avoid harassment and thus as a mask for disguising their 'real' opposition. To read it in this way ignores the possibility of genuine approval. Given the proletariat's initially low expectations of a National Socialist government, any favourable developments were all the more remarkable. Wages were low, but workers welcomed expanded vacation time, from seven to twelve days over the 1930s. Nazi welfare programmes and DAF relief provisions were appreciated. Workers also enjoyed newfound opportunities to take vacation trips with the DAF's Strength through Joy programme (see Chapter 2), while its Beauty of Labour schemes improved workplaces. The Nazis' attempts to integrate workers into national life, by appealing to them as good, patriotic Germans whose 'quality work' was valued, found favour.[25] Berlin's Tempelhof field, where mass festivities took place for the Day of German Labour on 1 May, filled with celebrants year after year.

Of course, participating in such events did not mean swallowing the Nazi message wholesale. Few German workers could resist a day off from work, with free drinks provided; some manoeuvred to avoid compulsory attendance or muttered criticism of the regime while there. Workers were not the truest believers in Nazism overall, but disciples of the *Führer* cult could certainly be found among them. Identity based on social class remained entrenched for some, while others were open to accepting an identity based on shared membership in the *Volksgemeinschaft*. By 1935, German workers in general were experiencing greater job security, possibilities for advancement and private happiness, which Weimar's crisis conditions had denied them. This fostered a more positive attitude, which, along with fear, minimized any open opposition. Most working-class Germans, whatever their personal convictions, were doing what the regime demanded of them: rebuilding and rearming the Reich.

The prospect of economic recovery encouraged middle-class support for the Nazis, even if these Germans had experienced lower rates of unemployment. The Great Depression hit unequally in 1929. While few suffered complete destitution, civil servants definitely felt the pinch of salaries reduced by austerity measures. The economic conditions of the traditional lower-middle class (*Mittelstand*) deteriorated even more drastically. By the end of the Weimar Republic, small shopkeepers, artisans and service providers (such as plumbers, photograph developers and auto mechanics) increasingly voted for the Nazis. Small businesses looked forward to Hitler's promised protection from department store competitors. Skilled craftsmen welcomed new opportunities through Nazi work creation schemes. However, once the real drive to rearmament began, the *Mittelstand* lost out: rearmament benefitted big business, not small enterprise. The department stores never closed down, although Jewish-owned ones were eventually 'Aryanized'. Many lower-middle-class Germans could still not afford what they made and services they provided. Resentment grew. In 1934, small shopkeepers moaned that 'nothing' had happened.[26] Salaried employees of private businesses did not see immediate and significant improvements in income or status either. The situation for upper-middle-class professionals – such as lawyers, doctors, dentists and engineers – was mixed. Although wages for civil servants remained depressed, general economic recovery improved the circumstances of individuals in private practice. Certain professions, physicians for example, enjoyed a marked increase in earnings with Hitler in power.

Private middle-class disappointments generally led to resignation, not open antagonism, for there was still much to applaud after 1933, particularly the regime's suppression of communism, something that scared middle-class Germans far more than the Nazis did. The 'Hitler Myth' – a belief in the *Führer* as a kind of semi-divine saviour and defender of the nation – was especially strong in their circles. They blamed the frustrations of daily life on the 'little Hitlers': Nazi Party functionaries and other officials. They enthused about the Third Reich's integration of Germans from all walks of life. A Hamburg schoolteacher, describing the Day of Potsdam as a 'momentous, unforgettably beautiful German day', noted how she cried tears of joy, alongside 'the grocer's wife, the cobbler's wife, the woman running the delicatessen'. Anyone who did not, she agreed, was 'not a real German'.[27]

From 1933, women like these became both targets and beneficiaries of Nazi propaganda and policies, which proclaimed and enforced traditional gender roles. While German men worked outside the home, women were to work within it as wives and mothers. The regime initially attempted to move women out of paid employment by forcing new brides to give up their jobs if their husbands had secure work. Many Germans, men and women, approved of such measures. Even in socialist and communist circles, complaints about so-called double earners had grown louder as the Great Depression worsened. To assist in setting up a household on a single income, the Nazis introduced Marriage Loans. These interest-free 1,000 *Reichsmark* loans, paid to the husband – not in cash but in certificates to be traded for furniture or household appliances at 'Aryan' stores – represented about two-thirds of an average worker's annual income. For each child, one quarter of the loan did not have to be repaid. With four children, the debt was cleared. The loans were thus meant to stimulate consumer spending and more general economic recovery, as well as the birth rate. Not surprisingly, 'non-Aryans', the politically 'unreliable', the disabled and those labelled 'asocial' were denied. The programme proved incredibly popular. By 1934, it contributed to an increase in marriage numbers and births spurred primarily by the overall improvement in economic conditions. As the economy recovered and the demand for labour grew, especially lower-paid female labour, more women returned to work without encountering consequences as 'double earners'.

Class significantly shaped the Nazi regime's impact on insider German women. Since a husband had to be able to support a family on one wage to qualify for a marriage loan, fewer working-class women went shopping with those certificates. Recognizing that most proletarian women had to work, by 1935 Nazi propaganda was back-pedalling on its stay-at-home messaging, proclaiming that women at their machines also served the nation. On paper, there was new protective legislation for mothers in factory and office jobs. In reality, this was rarely enforced; many working-class women put in sixty hours per week, and accident and miscarriage rates increased during the Third Reich.

By 1935, just like men, more women were working than during the Great Depression, though this varied by sector. The Nazis immediately forced women out of political office at all levels and prevented them from working in certain industries, such as mining. Female teachers had difficulty advancing their careers. Married female physicians lost the right to practice. By 1936, women could not legally serve as judges or public prosecutors. The Nazis nonetheless believed women had an essential role to play in fields like nursing, elementary school teaching and welfare services. To ensure women received the necessary training for such work, the regime reneged on its pledge to lower the number of female university students and their numbers increased.

Nazi auxiliary organizations provided further education on 'women's issues'. Membership in the National Socialist Women's Organization, the more elite, generally upper-middle-class Party organization, increased by 800 per cent over the course of 1933 to approximately two million. Four million eventually joined the

German Women's Bureau, the mass, middle-class variant; the Women's Department in the German Labour Front enfolded an additional five million mostly working-class women.[28] The Organization tended to focus on promoting Nazi ideology, while the Bureau and Department concentrated more on practical tasks women could perform for the nation. All three offered courses on things like housekeeping, childcare and cooking, alongside prenatal and parenting classes. There were lessons too on shopping frugally, buying German and making do with limited resources and scarce consumer goods. While their activities aimed at cementing Nazi ideas about women's roles within the *Volksgemeinschaft*, there was also some truth to Scholtz-Klink's post-war boast: monthly meetings, she claimed, afforded women some female autonomy since they offered a chance to gather 'without men', and to take on new leadership roles beyond the family circle.[29] These events had entertainment value as well, especially in small villages where little else was on offer.

The social welfare sphere offered additional incentives for women both as administrators and recipients of its programmes. In May 1933, the National Socialist People's Welfare Organization became the only official Party relief body; private and religious charities were disbanded or coordinated with it. Racial and social hygiene concerns motivated its efforts. 'Non-Aryan', 'unfit' and 'asocial' women and their families collected no assistance, while increased surveillance of the recipients made them vulnerable to persecution. Health and counselling services were also distributed unequally. Class and ability mattered. So-called brown nurses were relatively infrequent sights around proletarian neighbourhoods, and families with disabled children received far fewer visits. For others, though, the Welfare Organization provided genuinely appreciated material and emotional benefits.

Female insiders were thus both victims of a misogynist state and beneficiaries of its racist policies. Although constrained by a male-dominated regime, they were often able to carve out their own place, even in ways that opposed officially sanctioned principles. The regime's celebration of the homemaker role dovetailed with one already played by many German upper- and middle-class women. Their love for Hitler himself was often deep and abiding, and there was genuine belief among them in his promises of national renewal and an end to class war. Support in female working-class circles was less solid, but overall, 'women who satisfied the political, racial and social requirements' – the vast majority – 'did not perceive the Third Reich as a women's hell'.[30] In fact, as we see in later chapters, their positions inside the *Volksgemeinschaft* gave them power over those forced outside it.

Peasant farmers were essential for feeding that *Volksgemeinschaft*. During the 1920s, German farmers' share of the NSDAP vote had remained relatively small. When the Great Depression hit, although it affected agricultural sectors unevenly, foreclosures and mass indebtedness were common. Deeply conservative for the most part and virulently opposed to communism and socialism, the German peasantry felt more and more betrayed by the Weimar government, especially since it largely promoted exports of industrial – not food – products to effect economic recovery. The Nazis won them over with promises to restore vanished social prestige and make the agricultural sector more profitable, albeit without any concrete agrarian plans. Peasants thus played an active part in bringing Hitler to power. They expected great things of the new regime, while the regime expected great things from them in turn. Each was to be somewhat disappointed with the other. On the one hand, farmers – Catholics and Protestants – exulted at the regime's crackdown on the godless left. They applauded Germany's moves on the world stage, and often shared the antisemitic attitudes of the Party leadership in principle, if not always in practice. Farmers' faith in the *Führer* remained strong by 1935, and they largely exempted him from their criticism. On the other, the regime's new agricultural laws gave some cause for complaint.

The Hereditary Farm Law (1933) mandated state protection for any holding large enough to support a family adequately. It was to remain in the same family forever with only one child inheriting to avoid dividing the property. Foreclosures dropped, but the law was not universally popular since it also made borrowing money more difficult and imposed rules about managing the farms. German peasants also disliked elements of the Reich Food Estate, a body that oversaw all elements of food production, distribution and processing.

They resented having to sell only to it, with its fixed prices, when previously they sold directly to the consumer for potentially greater profit. As the regime worked out some of these first hiccups, however, complaints about the Food Estate grew less frequent and bitter.

The gendered nature of life on the land meant farmers' wives faced especially challenging circumstances. Combining agricultural work, childcare, meal preparation and cleaning left few free hours for rest or leisure. Harvest time meant even longer days. As men left the land, whether in search of higher-paid jobs in industry or through military conscription, women's burden became even heavier. In keeping with Nazi patriarchal ideas, the Hereditary Farm Law prioritized male relatives as heirs. Sons came first, then fathers and brothers before daughters and sisters; wives were forbidden from inheriting at all. Many male peasants expressed sharp criticism of the law's treatment of their wives. Few farm women had time to keep detailed diaries revealing their thoughts.

Exclusion from the line of inheritance contradicted the central role farm wives played in Nazi visual propaganda meant to boost the *Volk*'s fertility. Innumerable variations on Wolfgang Willrich's painting, *Family Picture*, appeared. Here, nature's bounty surrounds a blond haired, blue-eyed family. A farmer husband stands protectively over a mother with a baby at her breast, a son in HJ uniform and two daughters, one cradling a doll. Mass events like the Reich Harvest Thanksgiving Festival celebrated the peasantry every autumn outside Hamelin. Farmers' reactions to these events were mixed. In November 1935, the mayor of one town in the Magdeburg region reported, 'a large portion of the German peasantry looks upon the government and its measures with hostility'.[31] For every assessment like this, however, there is another praising the farmers' authentic embrace of Nazi ideology. Since the farming community actually fared better than the population as a whole between 1933 and 1935, their grumbling, criticism and even protests against specific policies rarely translated into a stance against the regime itself. When it did, it was often tied to religious confession, which further shaped supporters' responses to the regime.

Two-thirds of Germans were Protestants, and overall, Protestants warmly welcomed the coming of Hitler, praising the dawn of the Third

Figure 1.7 Wolfgang Willrich's painting, *Family Picture*, depicting an ideal 'Aryan' family (bpk Bildagentur/Wolfgang Willrich/Art Resource, New York).

Reich as a God-given miracle. Catholic Germans' embrace of the Third Reich was more hesitant at first. The Catholic Church forbade NSDAP, SA or SS membership until after the Concordat, an agreement signed between the Vatican and Nazi Germany in July 1933; thereafter,

Figure 1.8 Hitler shakes hands with Protestant Reich Bishop Ludwig Müller during the 1934 Nuremberg Party Rally. (Catholic) Nuremberg Cathedral is in the background and Catholic Abbot Alban Schachleiter stands between them (Daily Herald Archive/National Science & Media Museum/SSPL via Getty Images).

Catholics were still less likely to join an official Nazi organization. While 15–20 per cent of Protestant pastors were Nazi Party members, less than 1 per cent of Catholic clergymen were.[32] Yet Catholic distance from the regime should not be overemphasized. While Catholic Germans fought to maintain Church influence in schools and openly opposed the Sterilization Law, they did so while cheering the Nazis' achievements, including their campaigns against other outsiders. Christian faith thus proved generally compatible with an acceptance of Nazism, which allowed Nazi rule to be exercised as effectively in predominantly Catholic areas of Germany as in overwhelmingly Protestant ones.

How did 'ordinary' Germans generally respond to the Nazi persecution of those excluded from the *Volksgemeinschaft*? It was impossible to be completely unaffected by it; even attempting to withdraw or turn away involved a deliberate choice, albeit one made in the context of a brutal police state. Moreover, many German supporters – though clearly never all – accepted and justified the oppression unleashed on other Germans. Only when it became too visible or too violent did serious misgivings arise. It was therefore preferable when it erupted elsewhere – in Gestapo cells or concentration camps – and not in plain sight.

The majority of non-working-class Germans defended the Nazis' assaults on communists and socialists, especially after the Reichstag Fire. Curtailment of basic legal rights, even their own, was a small price to pay to suppress an alleged leftist revolt. Broad social consensus also emerged around the regime's treatment of racial and social outsiders, which gained widespread uncritical acceptance if not always direct approval. Here Nazi propaganda exacerbated existing prejudice and hostility rather than creating them. For example, its messages about the 'costs' of people with disabilities – to the race and the public purse – had long resonated with different parts of German society. Public objections to forced sterilization were exceedingly rare outside Catholic circles. Nazi propaganda also inflamed long-standing discriminatory attitudes towards 'asocials' and homosexuals. Legal measures against them seemed necessary to protect 'good' Germans.

Approving of persecution or even terror is one thing. Carrying it out is another. What role did 'ordinary' people play as perpetrators of violence in these years? Germans outside the SA, SS or police did not suddenly begin to beat up political opponents in 1933. While voluntary denunciations to the *Gestapo* added to the climate of suspicion and alarm, they did not play the leading, or even a very central, role in instigating the repression of the left. The *Gestapo* here was 'pro-active, not reactive', following information gained through interrogations or from other Party surveillance organizations rather than from informers' tips.[33] Left-leaning Germans thus had most to fear from Party officials – active, committed, loyal Nazis – not their neighbours. Supporters did bring the 'diseased', the 'asocial' and the sexually 'deviant' to the authorities' attention, but here too, the regime was usually more reliant on the official medical, judicial and police apparatuses than on 'ordinary' informants.

As for antisemitic persecution between 1933 and 1935, the story is more complicated, involving both top-down and bottom-up dynamics. It was clearly the Nazi Party leadership, at national and local levels, who initiated the opening movements of antisemitic terror in 1933; the male members of Nazi formations, especially the SA, were its primary perpetrators. The April 1933 boycott in particular was a Party-directed affair, one in which some Germans participated very energetically: posting signs, refusing to enter Jewish shops or visit Jewish doctors, and shouting abuse. Other Germans refused to march in step. Some bypassed SA and HJ sentries and went shopping. They apologized to Jewish business owners. They brought flowers to their Jewish doctors to express compassion. Continued business dealings and other interactions with Jewish Germans, should not, however, be understood as rejection of Nazi prejudice outright. Germans might protest injustices experienced by individual Jews, but almost never openly criticized the Third Reich's fundamental racism. The same applies to both the Catholic and Protestant churches, which never publicly protested the boycott or Nuremberg Laws, or indeed any antisemitic action or law between 1933 and 1935.

After the initial wave of anti-Jewish legislation and violence, 1934 was a relatively quiet year, at least in terms of open terror. This changed in 1935, when, buoyed by the increasingly stable foundations of the dictatorship, Party organizations at the local and regional level dramatically stepped up their anti-Jewish activism. This took the form of antisemitic boycotts, property damage, humiliations and physical assaults. These actions now gained broader public support. Signs saying 'Jews not wanted here' grew more common. Large crowds jeered as SA men and Hitler Youth shamed 'racial defilers', both Jews and 'Aryans'. At the same time, supporters feared such actions might be detrimental to economic recovery and foreign relations. Calls grew for state regulation of the 'Jewish Question'. Exploiting the popular mood, Hitler responded with the Nuremberg Laws in September 1935, which elicited a generally positive reaction. Legislation that codified relations between Jews and non-Jews was seen as a shrewd solution to an increasingly volatile situation. Supporters approved of this more 'respectable racism', removed from the streets but forced into 'offices, neighborhoods, schools and bedrooms'.[34] To police these more intimate spheres, the *Gestapo* and criminal police relied increasingly on denunciations about Jewish and 'Aryan' Germans being too friendly with one another. These undoubtedly led to more prosecutions for 'racial defilement'.

Nuremberg Laws

Hitler announced laws that codified the outsider status of 'non-Aryans' at the annual Nuremberg Party Rally on 15 September 1935. The first Reich Law of Citizenship divided *citizens* 'of pure German (or kindred) blood' from all others, who now became the Reich's *subjects*. The second Law for the Protection of German Blood and Honour prohibited marriage (and intimate relationships) between these two groups. Violations of that second law now became a crime, which the Nazis called 'racial defilement'. The Nuremberg Laws were the foundation for the Third Reich's avalanche of legislation against Jews, which excluded them from German economic, social and cultural life. The Laws also legitimated grassroots efforts – already underway in many locations – to segregate Jews from other Germans, including locally enforced bans on their entry to many public places.

Sometimes they led to the concentration camps. One of the most enduring questions about the Third Reich remains: What did Hitler's supporters know about what occurred in the camps? The question seems easier to answer for this early period because concentration camps were front-page news. The Nazis needed Germans to know about their existence for them to function effectively as a deterrent. At the same time, they worked to limit knowledge about actual camp conditions. Inmates agreed to say nothing about their experiences to gain their release and signed statements saying they had been treated well. The regime insisted that allegations circulating abroad about abuses were fake news. Certainly, few Germans imagined concentration camps as pleasant places. Yet deprivation and punishment were warranted, they reasoned, if these 'enemies' represented a real danger to the *Volk*. It is also important to recognize that Dachau in the spring of 1933 was not Auschwitz in 1942. Until 1935, the SA and SS camp guards followed some rules; the mass arbitrary violence and starvation of the later era were not yet present. Still, fear of the camps and other forms of Nazi 'justice' contributed to minimizing opposition, and reduced willingness to assist outsiders or protest their treatment.

Camps and Killing Centres in Nazi Germany

When the Nazi regime encountered a problem, the answer often came in the form of a camp. Camps were everywhere in the Third Reich, both within Germany and in the countries it conquered. The variety of camps was bewildering. There were labour camps and transit camps (used to hold victims temporarily before deportation elsewhere). There were camps for political opponents, juvenile offenders, hostile foreign workers and prisoners of war. Best known were the concentration camps. Under SS leader Heinrich Himmler's authority, they imprisoned political opponents and racial and social outsiders. While differing 'in size, conditions and function', concentration camps 'were united by a common aim to terrorize their inmates and intimidate the wider population'. By the end of the Second World War, the Nazi camp universe had incarcerated several million men, women and children, German and non-German. At least two million of them died there.[35]

In addition to these camps, during the Second World War the Nazis established six 'euthanasia' killing centres within the German Reich (Bernburg, Brandenburg, Grafeneck, Hadamar, Hartheim and Sonnenstein) and six death camps in occupied Poland (Auschwitz-Birkenau, Bełżec, Chełmno, Majdanek, Sobibór and Treblinka). With the exception of individuals selected for labour at the camps – vast numbers of whom were exterminated through work – this was a death sentence. Here victims were gassed, either with carbon monoxide or Zyklon B, a pesticide manufactured by a German company, IG Farben.

The Nazis' supporters could accept that violence was legitimate, even commendable, as long as it targeted the 'right' people and was not in the streets. They continued relations with outsiders when it was in their personal interests, especially economic ones, to do so. They were motivated on occasion to speak out openly against mistreatment of individual persecuted Germans – much more for disabled and Jewish Germans than for 'asocials' or homosexuals – but Interior Minister Wilhelm Frick was right: the old commandment to 'Love thy neighbour' was out of date in the new Germany.[36]

Racial and social outsiders

Nazi ideology cast Jews as the archetypal outsiders. In January 1933, approximately 525,000 Jews lived in Germany, making up less than 1 per cent of the total population of 67 million. The vast majority lived in larger cities; one-third lived in Berlin, the capital. Germany's Jews were overwhelmingly members of the middle class, working in the business and commercial sectors. Fewer than 2 per cent worked in agriculture. Most were German-born, but one in five were Eastern Jews (refugees from Eastern Europe, usually Poland), more likely to be impoverished industrial workers, small artisans and peddlers. Despite Nazi propaganda to the contrary, the Jews in Germany obviously did not act and think alike, but some generalizations can be drawn. Despite having suffered equally during the Great War and Weimar's perpetual crises, their support for the Republic was generally higher. They voted for liberal, centrist political parties, although some also backed parties on the far left and right. Most Jews in Germany maintained some sense of ethnic and religious community through attendance at synagogues, especially on the High Holidays, and by belonging to religious and secular Jewish organizations, from Orthodox to Zionist ones. At the same time, the majority were deeply patriotic and felt themselves to be thoroughly German. They spoke German not Yiddish (unlike the Eastern Jews), sent their children to German public schools and revered the great achievements of German culture.

From our vantage point in a post-Holocaust world, it is difficult to grasp that, at first, the situation for Jewish Germans under Hitler appeared uncertain and thus potentially navigable. Since the Nazi regime's antisemitic persecution was intermittent and yet an ever-present threat, hope could accompany fear in this period. Distinct waves of violent assaults and anti-Jewish legislation occurred in 1933 and the second half of 1935, bookending a relatively quiet, stable period in 1934 and early 1935. However, antisemitic pressures never disappeared once Hitler became Chancellor. They were constant but contradictory, and varied across the country and within different social spheres. There was no set pattern as to where, when or why Jewish Germans experienced the most unrelenting antisemitic harassment, intimidation, exclusion and violence. Such mixed signals made the decision whether to stay in Germany or flee an agonizing one. In 1933 alone, approximately 35,000 Jewish Germans left the country, but annual numbers declined thereafter.

Those who stayed faced a situation 'as unprecedented as it was unpredictable'.[37] As the regime immediately set its course for removing Jews from economic life ('de-Jewification') and transferring more of it into 'Aryan' hands ('Aryanization'), Jewish Germans met with undeniable financial pressures and increased unemployment. The 1933 Civil Service Law meant they could no longer work as teachers, professors, judges and in other government positions. Doctors, engineers, lawyers and all others employed by the state lost their jobs. Voluntary employment discrimination in the private sector followed. Jews were also banned from working in film, theatre, fine arts, literature, music and journalism by legislation that established a Reich Culture Chamber under Goebbels, to which only 'Aryans' could belong. Unemployment soared. The 1 April 1933 boycott provided further evidence of the regime's economic intentions and a clear confirmation of Jews' outsider status. Jewish Germans' diaries record outrage, sadness and fear about the future. In desperation, war veterans stood outside their shops with their medals on display. Sometimes this elicited sympathy, recalled one storeowner, but this was also the day he realized he was 'German no more'.[38]

While not all Jewish Germans experienced economic destitution in these years, robust economic health was not common. The Jewish community in Germany responded with charity initiatives, such as those of the Economic Assistance Network. While inadequate, this was remarkable work in the face of adversity. Funded by private donors, congregations and organizations abroad, the network offered emigration counselling, legal advice, short-term credit and long-term loans. It created a directory of Jewish-owned businesses to support, negotiated exemptions for 'privileged' Jews like veterans, helped find work in Jewish companies and provided vocational retraining. Additional Jewish charity programmes offered further assistance.

If economic worries dominated the everyday experiences of most Jewish Germans between 1933 and 1935, actual physical violence and terror did not, although the threat always remained. That bodily assaults on Jews began under a virulently antisemitic new government did not surprise them. The perpetrators' utter disregard for the rule of law did. Although women were not exempt from the attacks, the brutality mainly targeted male Jews and it operated overwhelmingly in public. In spring and summer 1933, Polish Jews living in Germany became the Stormtroopers' first Jewish victims. The SA beat them, stole from them and vandalized their businesses. An estimated 1,000 attacks on foreign Jews took place that year. Communist and socialist Jews were also special targets of Nazi terror in 1933. Other German Jews suffered physical abuse more rarely. Throughout 1934, antisemitic incidents tended to involve property more than persons. In spring and summer 1935, as we have seen, the Nazis returned to violence as a weapon against the Jews. Antisemitic agitation and terror increased dramatically.

Now the targets were no longer primarily foreign Jews or communist sympathizers but any Jewish German. The main perpetrators of antisemitic violence also changed. Chastened by the Night of the Long

Knives, the SA no longer played the leading role. The SS and Hitler Youth smeared slogans in red paint on Jewish-owned stores. Physical assaults by young boys were also frequent. Jewish Germans attacked in the months before the Nuremberg Laws were often accused of 'racial defilement'. Such allegations were not new, but they became more vicious. Flyers distributed in advance of one antisemitic riot in Berlin asked, 'Do you know that the Jew is raping your daughter, abusing your wife?'[39] Forced processions of alleged race traitors attracted hundreds of spectators. Pleas from Jewish community organizations begging government officials to restore a lawful state of affairs had no effect. After the Nuremberg Laws, charges of 'racial defilement', now officially illegal, skyrocketed. Life became even more dangerous for those in 'mixed' relationships. For now, only Jewish men were taken into custody; by 1937, Jewish women were as well. While some 'mixed' marriages ended, the majority persisted despite *Gestapo* interrogations and even imprisonment.

Jewish Germans rarely reacted to violent threats and attacks with physical force. They were few against many police officers, Party figures and crowds of onlookers. Already vulnerable, many hoped by responding passively they might avoid the much-publicized concentration camps. In theory, and according to the law, neither state nor local powers could incarcerate them there only 'as Jews' before 1938. In practice, authorities used flimsy political or criminal charges to justify their imprisonment. The first Jewish Germans in the camps were leftist political opponents of Nazism. The Nazis also detained Jewish Germans as supposed 'asocials', homosexuals, 'race defilers' or for other 'crimes'. No matter the official reason for their stay, Jews were singled out by guards for persecution, forcing them to endure especially back-breaking physical labour and severe punishments.

Despite the horrors facing Jewish Germans once Hitler became Chancellor, some believed they might be protected from antisemitic measures since the Nazi regime itself often sent mixed signals. For example, Jewish war veterans were initially exempt from Civil Service Law provisions. In 1935, they even received the Cross of Honour for having served in the Great War. Their exclusion from 'German' society was inevitable once the veterans' loophole closed in December that year. Exclusion was especially painful for children, barred now from the communal festivities that became a hallmark of life in the Third Reich. The experiences of discrimination, segregation and ostracism in schools, the sudden end to friendships and even bans on Hitler Youth membership were also uniquely heartbreaking to this age group.

One quarter of Jewish children attended Jewish schools by the end of 1933, but most remained in the public school system until 1935. Here too there were mixed signals. Some classrooms had separate seats for Jews. Teachers barred Jewish children from field trips and left them off prize lists. They demonized 'non-Aryan' surnames and facial features. Former friends ignored them. In response, students sometimes proudly announced their Jewishness or dared to leave assemblies during the singing of Nazi songs. Other survivors recall kind teachers and enduring connections with classmates despite the portraits of Hitler on the walls. Gender mattered here. Boys generally experienced more verbal taunts, threats and physical bullying on the playground than did girls. Boys also recognized that their visibly Jewish, circumcised bodies made them vulnerable. Physical attacks and humiliations on the streets by HJ and BDM members were common. Still, some Jewish German children longed to join these organizations and pestered their parents about why it was not possible. A seven-year-old boy wanted an Aladdin's lamp to grant his one wish: 'to be a Nazi'.[40]

Older Jewish youth had similar experiences at institutes of higher learning. Legislation in April 1933 enforced a quota on Jewish students, expelling some and limiting the intake of others. Jewish German postsecondary students were denied financial assistance and scholarships. They also faced harassment and bullying from classmates and professors' comments about 'inferior' races.

But who exactly was a Jew? Later amendments to the Nuremberg Laws eventually defined 'full Jews' as having at least three Jewish grandparents, or, if fewer, those belonging to the Jewish community or who were married to Jews. They also created the category of so-called mongrels (*Mischlinge*), Germans with a Jewish father, mother or grandparent. About 300,000 such individuals resided in the country in 1933 and they too were now subject to persecution. 'Full' Jews of the Christian faith and Germans with mixed ancestry felt doubly excluded: discriminated against but without Jewish organizations, friends or family to comfort them. They belonged, they felt, to no one.

Jewish German responses to the Nuremberg Laws varied. Some welcomed them as a means to reduce assimilation with non-Jews and inspire emigration from Germany. Others were saddened but were optimistic that a tolerable relationship between Jews and other Germans might now emerge. All hoped the Laws would end the uncontrolled violence and antisemitic actions that had preceded them. Jewish Germans were also united in feeling the Laws' negative impact, including those who had largely been shielded from persecution to this point. The criminalization of relations between Jews and other Germans resulted in increased public humiliation. The threat of incarceration grew. All Jewish Germans suffered from the ostensible ban on their presence in public spaces. Swimming pools, restaurants and parks, not to mention Hitler Streets, were off limits, despite no official Nazi edict preventing it. As more and more locations voluntarily posted 'Jews not welcome' signs, Jewish Germans were unsure how to behave in public. Should they, for example, give the 'German greeting', the 'Heil Hitler' salute? Cut off from friendships and connections with other Germans, their isolation increased. Loneliness is a common theme in Jewish Germans' reminiscences about this period. Looking back, one Holocaust survivor recalled how his friends hardly left their houses 'so they would not have to keep experiencing how people avoided them.' They were 'lonely, lonely.'[41]

Recovering the voices and experiences of non-Jewish racial outsiders in Nazi Germany is more difficult, since their correspondence and diaries – especially by those Germans labelled 'unfit' and 'asocial' – are extremely sparse. In the case of disabled Germans, the perpetrators did not wear brown or black shirts; they wore doctors' scrubs, nurses' uniforms and judges' red robes. As a first step to reviving the 'Aryan' race, the regime issued the Law for the Prevention of Hereditarily Diseased Offspring in 1933. The law forced sterilization on Germans considered to be afflicted with feeble-mindedness, schizophrenia, manic depressive psychosis, hereditary epilepsy, Huntington's chorea, hereditary deafness and blindness, severe physical deformities or acute

Figure 1.9 A sign reading 'Jews are not wanted in this place!', August 1935 (Hulton Archive/Getty Images).

alcoholism. The Hereditary Health Courts, consisting of a judge and two doctors, made decisions about individual cases, which healthcare workers brought to their attention. In the first four years, doctors sterilized 50,000 Germans. Women, who underwent tubal ligations, died at a higher rate than did men who had vasectomies. Ninety per cent of the programme's estimated 2,000 fatalities were women, who passed away either during the operation itself or due to inadequate post-operative care.[42] When a 1935 amendment forced abortion on pregnant women prior to surgery, there were even greater risks.

The majority of victims were not afflicted by a hereditary disease. Instead, they were classified as 'asocial', including Germans experiencing homelessness and addiction, prostitutes, unwed mothers and young offenders. The poor were significantly overrepresented here. The Nazis clearly used sterilization as a means to prune what they saw as diseased branches on the 'Aryan' family tree, and as a method of punishment and social control of those who deviated from accepted codes of behaviour. Germans considered too sick, infirm or dangerous did not require the procedure, since they were to be purged by life-long institutionalization in psychiatric hospitals at their families' expense.

The medical authorities and judges presumed the victims of forced sterilization did not grieve the loss of their fertility. They did. In 1934, an inmate at a psychiatric institution wrote about his sterilization experience to family members: 'It aggravates me to realize that I am sterile. … I feel so violated. … I spend many evenings crying.'[43] Psychiatric hospitals reported attempted suicides occurring before and after the operation. The regime discriminated against Germans with disabilities in other ways too. The 'unfit' could not receive marriage loans or child benefits, and were eventually prohibited from wedding altogether with the October 1935 Marriage Health Law. That same year, disabled Germans were banned from attending school, while their former classmates continued to solve math problems calculating the costs of caring for 'cripples' and the 'feebleminded'. Nazi propaganda about the racially inferior was everywhere. *Volk und Rasse* (People and Race), a mass-market illustrated magazine often found in doctors' waiting rooms, charged the 'hereditarily ill' with

Figure 1.10 German children at the Schönbrunn Psychiatric Hospital near Dachau, potential candidates for the Nazis' sterilization programme, in 1934 (Bundesarchiv, Bild 152-04-27/Friedrich Franz Bauer).

polluting the community. 'Documentaries' about inherited illness, such as Sins of the Fathers (1935) and The Inheritance (1935), which used footage shot in psychiatric asylums, preceded feature films in cinemas across the country.

Few sources reveal how such 'dangers' to the race felt about being targeted and we know even less about the experiences of the supposedly 'work shy' – the unemployed, beggars and homeless – who were especially vulnerable to large-scale police round ups. Beginning in September 1933, they were detained in workhouses, 'beggar camps', youth 'education' camps and psychiatric institutions, or coerced into forced labour. Equally difficult to reconstruct are the impressions of so-called habitual criminals under Hitler, Germans convicted of multiple crimes. In November 1933, the regime passed the Law against Dangerous Habitual Criminals, which allowed for 'preventative detention' of serial offenders. Judges sentenced the most 'incorrigible' among them to indefinite confinement in prisons or workhouses after completion of their original sentence. Some 'habitual criminals' were sterilized; accused sex offenders could be castrated. Many suffered deep depression about incarceration without end, what one female inmate called a 'slow suicide'. Drastic weight loss, self-mutilation and self-harm attempts were frequent. The vast majority had been convicted for petty property offenses largely committed during Weimar's hard times of hyperinflation and depression, such as thefts of bicycles, coats or small amounts of food or money. Most were men, but there were women like Rosa S., a pickpocket and sometime prostitute, who dreamed of buying a sewing machine after leaving prison. Although an end to imprisonment was theoretically possible for such 'criminals' in the early years of the Third Reich, Rosa S. was never released.[44]

Until the Nuremberg Laws, the regime's persecution of other 'racial aliens' – for example, Black Germans and Sinti and Roma Germans – was more haphazard and inconsistent. Later chapters explore their stories. By contrast, its measures against another perceived threat to the *Volksgemeinschaft*, homosexual men, radicalized steadily from 1933. Himmler in particular was obsessed with rooting out gay men from society. He demonized them as effeminate paedophiles who not only failed to breed for the Nazi state but were potentially disloyal to it as well. Lesbians were not officially persecuted for homosexuality but for deviant 'asocial' behaviour. Police raids on gay pubs, bars and social clubs began immediately in 1933. While fear was constant, there were 'still possibilities for us to meet', one male gay survivor recalls, if not in public.[45] Once the regime charged the SA with homosexuality to justify the Night of the Long Knives murders, police persecution accelerated. In 1935, an amendment to existing legislation against homosexual behaviour (Paragraph 175) criminalized all 'indecent' acts, beyond intercourse alone.

Some pockets of relative tolerance endured in these early years. Several gay-friendly bars in Hamburg stayed open with hardly any official harassment and some actors and directors known to be gay retained their roles on stage and screen. Moreover, until the Night of the Long Knives, same-sex desiring men who considered themselves Nazis could believe they had a place in the Third Reich. Gay war veterans wrote to Hitler to express their support for national revival. Others highlighted and protested their mistreatment in anonymous letters to the authorities. These achieved little and perhaps even endangered the writers and their contacts. Since the majority of Germans shared traditional prejudices against homosexuals, the regime did not need to fear any open protests on their behalf.

Resisters

Germans who actively resisted Hitler between 1933 and 1935 – those who became outsiders by choice rather than force – represented a very small proportion of the population. They had certain things in common, at least in terms of whom the Nazis arrested for treason and high treason. First, the vast majority were young and middle-aged adults (roughly twenty to fifty). Second, they were almost all men. Third, although individual resisters came from across the political spectrum and social classes – even from the outset a few conservatives defied the Nazis – in terms of numbers, they were overwhelmingly left-wing and working-class. Finally, resisters rarely cooperated across political factions, classes or faiths, something that greatly hindered chances of success.[46]

Hitler recognized that the left-wing parties, especially the communists, posed the major danger to his new government. By February 1933, it was already illegal for the German Communist Party to hold meetings, demonstrate publicly or publish its views. The Reichstag Fire Decree authorized indefinite detention in 'preventive custody' for political enemies without due legal process. Their actions became treason, a crime that carried the death penalty. State-sanctioned Nazi terror swept over German communists, with SA men more than the *Gestapo*, police or SS leading the way. Brownshirts kidnapped, beat up, tortured and murdered communists, both on the streets in full public view and in other 'sites of extralegal detention', including sports centres, unused factories, old hotels, restaurants and taverns.[47] Ernst Thälmann, Party Chairman since 1925, was arrested in Berlin in March 1933; he spent eleven years in solitary confinement in a German prison before his execution in Buchenwald concentration camp in 1944. Other principal functionaries quickly fled abroad. By

Figure 1.11 Communists arrested by the SS in Düsseldorf, 1933 (ADN-Bildarchiv/ullstein bild via Getty Images).

March 1935, almost all remaining communist leaders in Germany had been arrested or executed.

This extraordinarily violent suppression met with stubborn, energetic resistance. Given that armed insurrection was impossible with the SA and the military behind Hitler, and that attempted mass actions like demonstrations and strikes were brutally crushed, activity turned largely to readying the Communist Party for power. It was only a matter of time, communists believed, before the wheels of history moved in their favour. Fascism, the apogee of capitalism, would crumble and the dictatorship of the proletariat could begin. It was critical to keep membership loyal in the interim through propagandistic writings such as flyers, newspapers and leaflets. Some were smuggled in from abroad, others printed clandestinely on German presses. In 1935 alone, German communists distributed an estimated one million illegal leaflets. Sabotage efforts on the factory floor were infrequent, but resilience showed itself in red flags flying from chimneys in working-class neighbourhoods and in anti-Nazi slogans daubed in white paint. Yet these highly visible signs of resistance only led to more terror. German communists went into survival mode, meeting in smaller circles with fewer contacts between them. By 1935, the most heroic phase of communist resistance was already over.

Despite pledging to oppose Nazism as the Third Reich began, members of Germany's Social Democratic Party resisted Hitler's regime less actively and persistently than communists did. Its chairman, Otto Wels, fled Berlin for Prague in May 1933. There he established a leadership in exile (SOPADE), which he served until his death in Paris in 1939. German socialists found the transition to illegal struggle thoroughly disorienting. For fourteen years, they had been the staunchest supporters of the Weimar state. Now they too faced full-blown Nazi terror. As with the communists, it combined the SA's extra-legal avenues and, increasingly, 'legal' *Gestapo*, police and judicial actions. Men and women had their flats invaded and faced brutal interrogations accompanied by physical beatings. Prominent socialist politicians were kidnapped, sent to concentration camps and tortured to death. SA thugs arrested 500 Berlin socialists during a single week in June 1933 and murdered almost one-fifth of them.[48] The Social Democratic Party was outlawed the same month.

Some resistance by smaller socialist groups persisted, but most chose to stop all political activities. These Germans kept their views secret, maintaining only loose contacts, if any, with former associates. Concern about employment and not wanting to be excluded often facilitated at least an outward conversion to a new political ideology. A relative few lived a double life and planned for a socialist future after the collapse of Hitler's rule. This meant small clandestine meetings and communication with SOPADE, rather than the broad dissemination of anti-Nazi propaganda, although publications did circulate underground. For the historian, the most important socialist resistance activity was SOPADE's compilation and publication of the *Reports from Germany*, secret reports on German workers' morale and attitudes to Nazism, which carried on until 1940. Already by the end of 1935, however, the Nazis had liquidated all real leftist threats to their hold on power.

Communists and socialists opposed the fascist Nazi regime as a whole. For other Germans who generally supported the Third Reich, specific policies triggered dissent. Those with family members at risk of sterilization soon clashed with authorities. Parents of children reported to the Hereditary Health Courts wrote letters expressing their opposition, swearing not to hand them over for the operation. While this ultimately failed to protect most victims, familial protest could sometimes at least postpone the procedure, as could formal court appeals. The most open and concerted opposition to sterilization came from Catholics, both the clergy and lay people. The Pope himself condemned it as unnatural interference in God's plans. Their efforts had some impact. The regime exempted Catholic doctors from performing sterilizations or from having to sign the orders for them. Yet the Church itself also backed down. Catholics could and should, it decided, report patients deemed 'unfit' to reproduce.

Once the programme was in full operation, Catholic opposition to it varied. Nursing sisters at certain Catholic psychiatric institutions refused to accompany patients to the procedure. Others coached their charges on the acceptable answers to standardized intelligence tests, administered before the Health Court judges gave their verdicts. These included questions ranging from 'How do you plan your future?' to 'Who is Martin Luther?'[49] Protestant health care workers, generally more tolerant of Nazi eugenic practices, engaged in far fewer such actions. In the end, however, compliance rates did not significantly differ between Catholic and Protestant regions. Any objections ultimately had little impact on the number of sterilization operations performed.

Other conflicts between the German churches and the Nazi regime flared up in these early years, including the Protestants' so-called Church Struggle. This was not a struggle by Protestants against the Hitler state, as the name might imply, but an internal conflict between different types of Protestants. By late 1933, anger had grown at government efforts to unify Germany's forty-five million Protestants within a single evangelical Reich Church led by Bishop Ludwig Müller, an ardent Nazi who called himself a 'stormtrooper for Christ'.[50] In response to this attempted forced coordination, several pastors now founded a movement called the Confessing Church, which around one third of Protestant pastors eventually joined.[51] One of its leaders was Martin Niemoeller, a staunch nationalist who had warmly greeted Hitler's new government and was still generally supportive of the Third Reich. As irritating as his Confessing Church was, the regime made no move to outlaw it, but it did punish individual pastors for speaking out against the Nazis' interference in religious matters. Niemoeller himself was arrested in January 1934. Freed due to widespread protests on his behalf, he was permanently suspended from preaching. Nonetheless, the seeds of the Confessing Church as a platform for future resistance had been planted.

For racial and social outsiders, individual and community efforts to preserve and defend themselves became forms of resistance. Sterilization candidates, for example, tried various means of self-assertion before the Hereditary Health Courts. One defendant even composed a poem for the judge, describing the sorrows and distress of the mentally ill.[52] However, the 'unfit' were doubly damned when they stood up for themselves. It showed the authorities that they did not understand the racial health issues involved, thereby proving their mental weakness. Once sentenced to sterilization, victims regularly ignored the written summons to appear until they were taken forcibly to the clinics. Protest pregnancies were a deliberate attempt to thwart a sterilization sentence by conceiving. These occurred often enough that the Sterilization Law was amended in 1935 to authorize abortion in such cases. One woman said she had gotten pregnant 'to show the state that I won't go along with this'.[53]

With the exception of physically disabled Germans (see Chapter 2), collective opposition by those labelled 'inferior' and 'asocial' did not occur, although Catholic Germans protested together on their behalf. No German resistance group put opposition to Nazi antisemitism at the core of its activities and no exclusively Jewish resistance organization emerged before the war's outbreak. Yet Jewish Germans defied the Nazis individually and also resisted as members of underground leftist organizations. Herbert and Marianne Baum, for example, lived in a working-class neighbourhood in Berlin. They belonged to both the German Jewish Youth Community and the Communist Youth League, and were committed to staying in Germany to try to topple Hitler. Between 1933 and 1935, the so-called Baum group wrote pamphlets denouncing the regime, detonated 'leaflet bombs' in the Berlin State Library and distributed an anti-fascist newspaper. One issue exhorted: 'Love your country, think for yourself – a good German is not afraid to say "no".'[54]

Jewish self-help organizations resisted Nazi intentions by mitigating Jewish distress, if not by opposing Nazi orders. The National Representation of German Jews, founded in September 1933 under Rabbi Leo Baeck, was the central body coordinating care and protection for the Jewish community. It discouraged emigration and expressly criticized militant, illegal or subversive anti-Nazi activities, fearing collective vengeance and deterioration of an already precarious position. After the war, organizations like these were accused of helping maintain the fantasy that some kind of normal life might still be possible for Jews in Nazi Germany. However, by seeking to minimize suffering, their efforts still challenged the Nazis' attempt to impoverish and shatter. The Jewish Culture League offered a different avenue for cultural resistance, even though it was established by the Nazis themselves in the summer of 1933 and was led by an 'old fighter' reporting to Goebbels. Jewish artists, funded by the Jewish community, performed exclusively for Jewish audiences. Regional Jewish culture leagues ran equivalent operations across the country, all under the auspices of what by 1935 had become the Berlin-based Reich Association of Jewish Culture Leagues. Some 70,000 members in forty-nine different locations undertook all kinds of activity.[55] There were plays, concerts and lectures; publishing and film projects were even completed. The regime controlled programming content – German composers like Beethoven were prohibited to 'un-German' Jews – and the *Gestapo* guaranteed compliance. Was the Association guilty as charged of complicity in camouflaging Nazi oppression? Unintentionally, perhaps, but its activities also provided jobs for unemployed artists, a temporary reprieve from the harsh realities of daily life and an 'opportunity to remain creative and productive amidst the great struggle for basic survival'.[56]

Although we will never know the names of all German resisters, it bears repeating that those who opposed Nazi measures or engaged in deliberate, anti-Nazi activities were exceedingly few, even during the beginnings of the Third Reich. Their 'no' – either to specific Nazi policies or to the Nazi state itself – was drowned out by many more expressing an active or passive 'yes'.

CHAPTER 2
THE 'GOOD OLD DAYS' (1936–1937)

Throughout 1936 and 1937, Germany became increasingly Nazified; at the same time, Nazism – its passions, its hatreds, its achievements and its threats – grew more normalized. Goose-stepping German soldiers grabbed world attention when they marched into the Rhineland on 7 March 1936. With the remilitarization of the region, a bold violation of the Treaty of Versailles, Hitler had taken an aggressive step towards realizing his goals. He made further progress by securing international agreements with countries friendly to fascism and hostile to communism. In autumn 1936, the regime announced the economic Four Year Plan under Hermann Goering. It had two basic goals: autarky (economic self-sufficiency) and war preparedness. From now on, foreign and economic policy in the Third Reich overwhelmingly centred on and served the Nazis' drive to war. Nonetheless, international visitors arriving for the 1936 Winter and Summer Olympic Games returned home with predominantly positive impressions of the new Germany under the swastika.

Domestically, the regime worked to regularize past Nazi initiatives and bring additional areas of German life in line with National Socialist ideals and aims. Once considered temporary tribunals, the People's Courts became permanent institutions in April 1936. In June, the SS gained substantial new powers of 'legal' persecution with Heinrich Himmler's appointment as Chief of German Police, which centralized SS control over all German police forces. The Nazi concentration camp universe expanded in these years. New major camps opened, which now interned Sinti and Roma, homosexual and so-called 'asocial' Germans in greater numbers, alongside new categories of inmates. The prisoner population overall began to rise again even though active political resistance was at an all-time low.

Towards the end of this phase, in July 1937, Nazi visions for German culture were celebrated at the first annual Great German Art Exhibit in a new House of German Art in Munich. The nazification of German culture was well underway, and Hitler's favourite architect, Albert Speer, emerged as a newly influential henchman ready to serve the *Führer*'s grand designs. On 5 November 1937, an important meeting took place between Hitler, his senior military commanders and the Foreign Minister. Hitler revealed his strategy and timeline for the conquest of *lebensraum* (living space) by force, beginning with Austria and Czechoslovakia sometime between 1943 and 1945. In his mind, though, the possibility of earlier military action remained open.

Nazis

The Nazis, none more than the *Führer* himself, showed increasing self-confidence and renewed determination to reach their ideological goals in these years. There was a marked shift in Hitler's focus, from inner-Party concerns and domestic issues, to foreign policy matters. In those, he was now much more inclined to gamble, as with the remilitarization of the Rhineland. As Hitler grew ever more assertive, ignoring the concerns of conservative state ministers and generals, his diplomacy became more aggressive. He solidified an alliance with Fascist Italy and made overtures to Japan, resulting in the tripartite Anti-Comintern Pact in 1937. Along with highlighting his hostility to the Soviet Union, the Pact showed that Hitler was abandoning his former dreams of a partnership with Great Britain. His readiness to challenge socialism and communism beyond Germany was revealed by his deployment of the German Air Force to assist Francisco Franco's Nationalists during the Spanish Civil War. Emboldened on the international stage, Hitler began to consider riskier solutions to the 'Jewish Question' at home. Addressing 800 Party leaders on the topic in late April 1936, he reassured his audience he knew what he could get away with and what he could not: 'I always go to the very brink of boldness but not beyond.'[1] The *Führer*'s belief in his own infallibility was an important factor in radicalizing economic policy and reorienting it for war. As always, he set vague goalposts for others to 'work towards' – autarky and intensified rearmament in the case of the Four Year Plan – without himself becoming mired in the details. Yet he also remained sensitive to popular opinion and intervened personally whenever national unity might be at stake. By late 1937, Hitler felt more secure than ever to pursue a distinctly Nazi foreign policy, propelled by a nazified economy, and to deal decisively with any obstacles in his way.

Four Year Plan

Hitler announced the Four Year Plan, a plan for steering Germany's economic development, at the annual Nazi Party Rally in Nuremberg in September 1936. Its aim was to make Germany industrially independent and more agriculturally self-sufficient to prepare the country for war. Hermann Goering became its overlord. The Plan focused primarily on rearmament and increasing the production of synthetic rubber and fuels, but it initiated diverse public works and building projects as well. It was renewed in 1940 for the duration of the war.

Himmler significantly expanded his powers over the policing of society and the enforcement of racial 'security' in this period. In June 1936, he became Reich Leader SS and Chief of German Police in the Ministry of Interior, thereby uniting Party and state offices in his hands, just as Hitler was *Führer* of the Party and Reich Chancellor of the state. For now, Himmler was technically subservient to the Interior Minister, and he continued to butt heads with other Reich ministries. Yet his personal obsessions and hatreds – Christianity, 'Gypsies', homosexuals and youthful non-conformity in particular – increasingly determined which outsiders would suffer alongside Jews, 'asocials' and political resisters. He also shaped where they suffered: in an enlarged, fundamentally reorganized system of concentration camps over which he and the SS would exclusively preside. The small, widely dispersed 'protective custody' camps were already largely dissolved; two big new camps took their place, Sachsenhausen (1936) and Buchenwald (1937). There, SS guards adopted practices first employed at Dachau, the Nazis' 'model camp'. Inmates now wore coloured, triangle-shaped badges for the first time. These literal signifiers of their outsider status, marking out their various 'crimes', dehumanized them and segregated them from one another, minimizing the potential for collective resistance.

With the growth of Himmler's SS empire, new organizations were tasked with finding solutions to the 'Jewish Question', including Adolf Eichmann's department for Jewish affairs within the Security Service. Overall expansion brought the SS to approximately 215,000 men by 1937. Only 5,000 or so belonged to the Death's Head units at this time, members of whom served as guards and administrators at the concentration camps. The vast majority – 90 per cent – were in the so-called General SS, consisting of a small number of professional leaders and a large group of voluntary members.[2] These 'ordinary', lower-ranking SS men often wore the black uniform only part-time and combined weekly meetings, drills, educational courses and charitable initiatives with fulltime careers elsewhere. Many saw advantages to SS membership, which allowed otherwise unremarkable men to climb the career ladder, especially within German policing organizations. Still, professional advancement was inseparable from commitment to an elite institution, one that embodied Nazi ideological ambitions and primary loyalty to Hitler.

From 1936 to 1937, Hermann Goering was at the height of his power. His *Luftwaffe* showed promise assisting the Nationalists during the Spanish Civil War. More importantly, as head of the Four Year Plan, he was instrumental in setting Germany's economy firmly on the path to war with almost dictatorial powers to ensure success. He was in charge of all matters concerning foreign exchange, raw materials and rearmament generally. Despite his ignorance in economic affairs and a reputation for lavish spending – the opposite of what the Four Year Plan preached to German consumers – Goering had shown himself to be ruthless and loyal. For Hitler, that was enough. His good contacts within the German business community were an added

Figure 2.1 SS men on parade, 1936 (MARKA/Alamy Stock Photo).

bonus. Thus, he remained in the *Führer's* graces despite his support for coming to an agreement with Great Britain long after Hitler had abandoned that option, and openly admitting his belief that Hitler's timeline for war with the Western powers was unrealistic. Goering won battles with Economics Minister Schacht and generals in the War Ministry over economic jurisdiction, and established himself as an industrial leader with the colossal state-owned enterprise Reich Works Hermann Goering, which extracted and produced domestic iron ore. He clearly relished his victories. Named interim Economics Minister after Schacht was dismissed in 1937, Goering telephoned him to announce gleefully: 'I am now sitting in your chair!'[3]

Propaganda Minister Joseph Goebbels also fortified his power base in these years, extending and tightening his hold on the cultural sphere. His earlier propaganda efforts had largely focused on stabilizing the regime and promoting more positive images of Germany abroad. Those continued, but he also launched a concerted attack on the supposed immorality of the Catholic Church and renewed antisemitic messaging. Goebbels's top priority, though, was nazifying German culture; radio programming, the press and the German film industry all came under the Ministry of Propaganda's control. What would and would not be acceptable in the future became clearer with every step, especially with regard to the visual arts. Despite an earlier appreciation for Expressionism, Goebbels spearheaded the Degenerate Art Exhibition in Munich in 1937 – held across the street from the Great German Art Exhibition – to show he shared Hitler's artistic tastes. Modernism was to be exterminated.

As these leading Nazis' stars rose, new figures became increasingly influential. Albert Speer, a young, ambitious architect, was poised to become Nazi Germany's foremost master builder. His neoclassical style – with a particular fondness for the stone columns that defined Nazi architecture – meshed well with the *Führer*'s aesthetics. Named General Building Inspector for the Reich Capital in 1937, his attention turned to reshaping the physical face of Berlin, to be renamed Germania, in accordance with Hitler's wishes. The rather talentless Joachim von Ribbentrop, head of the Party's bureau for foreign affairs, also grew closer to Hitler. As Ambassador to Great Britain from 1936, he nipped at von Neurath's heels, jostling for more power in diplomatic circles.

Triumphs like the Rhineland amplified Hitler's approval ratings among high-ranking Party functionaries and solidified their support. In return, Hitler was fiercely loyal to them. Only one of the thirty-one *Gauleiter* (Regional Leaders) lost his position in these years, and even he was later rehabilitated. Although their authority paralleled rather than supplanted that of state leaders (in some cases *Gauleiter* functioned in both capacities as Reich Governors), they managed, as one acknowledged, to 'make quite a lot' of their station, albeit 'largely outside the legal limits'.[4] They appointed Party men to government roles and pursued populist strategies, urging citizens to come to them with complaints against other authorities. Their push for economic legislation on the ground radicalized national policy in turn, especially with regard to 'de-Jewification'. Corrupt Party officials prospered personally as well. They skimmed from various funds and benefitted from the dispossession of Jewish Germans via pseudo-legal measures. Party functionaries with state roles also led the way in instigating the outbursts of supposedly popular antisemitism that did occur in these relatively quiet years.

The Nazi Party gained an even more prominent presence in German society with the 1936 restructuring of its formations. Local branches were subdivided into smaller units called cells and blocks. Their leaders, a new cadre of lowly, but devout, Party members, were expected to 'uncover and expose unhealthy ideological developments' in every neighbourhood and every street.[5] They were to observe and report on everything from unsatisfactory marriages, poor parenting and pregnancies, to business practices, and were widely resented for their constant spying. Some Block Wardens were frustrated by their relatively menial duties, but they did have power over other Germans' lives, since keeping secrets from them was often more difficult than hiding them from the *Gestapo*.

The period from 1936 to 1937 represented the low point of SA activities, influence and membership, which was down 40 per cent according to some estimates. The pause on new, more radical antisemitic measures was disillusioning for remaining Stormtroopers who liked to chant, 'Once the Olympics are through, we'll beat up the Jew!'[6] While violent assaults had to wait, the resurgence of antisemitic propaganda towards the end of 1937 reassured many that solving the 'Jewish Question' was still on the agenda. As the SA shrunk, the Hitler Youth grew. On 1 December 1936, it became the official state youth organization. Membership was not yet mandatory, but it was widely perceived to be. With their own groups now dissolved, Catholic youth joined in greater number. At the same time, intensified indoctrination in school and extracurricular activities pushed children to embrace the regime's world view. There were even special 'Adolf Hitler Schools' to nurture fledgling Party leaders, Germany's future elite.

Accomplices

Individually, the old German elites expressed certain misgivings about the Nazi regime – its attacks on Christianity made them uneasy, as did blatant violations of the rule of law – but as a group, they made no serious break with it. In January 1937, a second Civil Service Law intensified the coordination of the country's public servants at the Reich, state, county and municipal levels by demanding more concrete evidence of political loyalty. Civil servants, just like *Wehrmacht* soldiers, had to swear an oath to Hitler. Far more than before, promotion to higher office hinged on evidence of ideological reliability. Unbecoming conduct, by them or their family members, such as shopping at Jewish stores, was grounds for dismissal. So too was a 'non-Aryan' spouse. To prove their loyalty and further safeguard their positions, key elites like Justice Minister Franz Gürtner, Foreign Minister Konstantin von Neurath and War Minister Werner von Blomberg joined the Nazi Party in 1937 when party rolls opened for the first time since 1933.

Yet, even now, Party membership was not essential for retaining a post. Economics Minister Hjalmar Schacht remained an 'honourary member' only, and by the end of 1937, only half of University Chairs had joined. Industrialists and landowners did not suddenly enrol in any significant numbers. Therefore, despite recognizing that the Nazis held the balance of power, Germany's traditional elites believed there was still room to manoeuvre, to pursue individual interests and agendas, and even express dissenting opinions. Certain privileges were preserved and additional ones gained. Foreign policy successes, economic improvement based on rearmament and spectacles like the Olympics further bound them to the regime. Their domains remained, if not always bastions of Nazism, then certainly not bulwarks against it.

There were concrete perks to be had. Academics exploited growing fields of study, offering theories about German racial and cultural superiority, while advancing their own careers. In university medical faculties, eugenic 'science' melded especially easily with Nazi obsessions. Curricula changed to give future doctors more training in assessing hereditary diseases and symptoms of racial inferiority. Newly established, state-funded research institutes, such as the Institute for Hereditary Biology and Racial Hygiene in Frankfurt, offered positions to men like Dr Josef Mengele. The Reich Institute for the History of the New Germany supported regime-friendly historians. Other scholars, from archaeologists to geologists, found employment in Himmler's Ancestral Heritage think tank. The Nazis wanted experts on rearmament and autarky, and sought the advice of university-trained technocrats. German doctors, well over one-third of whom joined the Nazi Party, were enjoying the highest income of any professional group in the country, and gained in social status as well.[7] They used their academic credentials to confer legitimacy on the Nazi racial project by issuing certificates permitting Germans to marry and testifying to the need for sterilization in Health Courts.

With the People's Courts now permanent, their judges were able to don the prestigious red robes previously reserved for the Supreme Court judiciary. They responded to the privilege by issuing more severe sentences against the *Volk*'s enemies. At times, German judges, and Justice Minister Gürtner himself, tried to defend their authority against increasing encroachment by the extralegal elements of the police state, as when the *Gestapo* hauled defendants found innocent straight to concentration camps. In truth, there was usually more collaboration than competition between the judiciary and Nazi organizations. Treason files, for example, were regularly exchanged between the *Gestapo*, prosecutors and People's Court judges.

Nazi successes in foreign policy served the individual career interests of the German military elite as well. Promotions followed the remilitarization of the Rhineland, including War Minister Blomberg to Field Marshal. Blomberg had supported Hitler's deployment of troops across the Rhine, but men like Werner von Fritsch, the German Army's Commander-in-Chief, objected to its risky timing, if not the goal itself. The success of the gamble renewed their faith in the *Führer*, while their previous timidity increased his contempt for them. Goering's control over rearmament via the Four Year Plan still frustrated the generals since they wanted to oversee all aspects of war preparation. Tensions over resource shortages and allocation, industry priorities and other elements of the war economy simmered.

At what became known as the Hossbach meeting on 5 November 1937 (so named because Friedrich Hossbach, a German staff officer, later drafted a memorandum about it), Hitler addressed Germany's current diplomatic situation at length – the Foreign Minister was also present – and prospects for future armed conflict. That Hitler saw *lebensraum* as the solution to Germany's economic problems was no surprise, but his readiness to consider military action as early as the next year was. His commanders knew the German *Wehrmacht* was not, and would not be, ready by 1938 for war against France and Britain should they choose to oppose Hitler's aim to seize Austria and Czechoslovakia. Disquiet among the armed forces leadership had little impact. It remained overwhelmingly loyal to Hitler and supportive of the Third Reich, but a small minority had shown their hand. There were consequences for their reluctance to follow the *Führer* unconditionally.

Von Neurath and other top-level diplomats in the Foreign Office generally agreed with the direction of Hitler's foreign policy following the Rhineland victory – expanding in Central Europe by way of Austria, breaking up Czechoslovakia and revising the Polish frontier – but they questioned how this could be done without risking war or increasing German isolation. Von Neurath in particular feared endangering relations with Great Britain. Yet he willingly played along. Relations between the regime and the head of the Economics Ministry, Schacht, were on much shakier ground. Schacht believed in foreign trade and acquiring colonies, not total autarky and the aggressive pursuit of European living space. As Goering's control over the militarized economy expanded, Schacht was increasingly sidelined. The Hossbach meeting in November 1937 sent a final warning to Schacht and conservatives like him: Hitler would tolerate no more opposition. He sacked Schacht as Economics Minister later that month, replacing him with Goering. Total commitment to the Four Year Plan was now guaranteed.

The Four Year Plan placed much tighter limits on industrial autonomy. Meeting its production targets was difficult due to shortages of required raw materials and the poor quality of domestic substitutes. Business elites criticized state-set prices, wage levels and foreign currency regulations as well. Huge government contracts came to those willing to pursue the Nazis' goals, however, and there were new areas for growth and private investment, especially within industries critical to the goal of autarky. For established men of industry, there were avenues for further advancement heading departments charged with implementing the Four Year Plan. Moreover, companies like IG Farben were genuinely excited about technological innovations unrealizable in a 'normal' economy. When carrots alone failed to motivate compliance, the sticks appeared. A new law against economic sabotage, such as acquiring raw materials not linked to the Four Year Plan, carried the death penalty. Landed aristocrats anxiously watched as the Nazis' focus on rearmament drained labour from the rural economy, although the impact on larger estates was often less severe than on smaller peasant farms, especially since, from 1937 onwards, they received the majority of all newly arriving voluntary foreign workers.

There was no significant opposition among Germany's traditional elites to the regime's persecution of outsiders. In fact, their support for Nazi racial policy encouraged its radicalization. The Justice Ministry was not alone in expanding racial legislation without orders from the top; indeed, nearly all ministries devised new statutes, largely on their own initiative. The military leadership itself demanded wider application of racist laws. Big business yielded easily to Nazi pressures to widen and increase the tempo of 'de-Jewification' and 'Aryanization'. 'Aryan' buyers bought up Jewish firms, including larger enterprises like banks and factories. In elite circles, benefits like these tended to offset any grievances.

Supporters

Attitudes to the Third Reich among the German majority appear particularly paradoxical in this period. Some historians have highlighted popular discontent in early 1936, citing secret reports on the negative public mood, diminishing enthusiasm for mass Nazi events and other symptoms of dissatisfaction, like the disappearance of the 'Heil Hitler' greeting in some locations. At the same time, there is good evidence that the majority of Germans, then and later, considered these years the start of 'good times' which, for some, even outlasted the outbreak of war, and propelled them to become Hitler supporters if they were not already.[8] How do we reconcile such contradictions?

First, in this context, seasonal fluctuations played a role. The popular mood in the Third Reich responded to material conditions: it dipped over the winter 1935/1936, when fat shortages loomed and food prices climbed, but rose again by the summer as employment soared and consumer goods grew more affordable. Second, grumbling about everyday concerns does not indicate wholesale disenchantment with the regime. There was often consensus about the big picture alongside complaints about the little one. Finally, as Nazism became 'normal', some Germans' earlier excitement and euphoria faded, while ambivalence increased. This explains, at least partially, the increasingly lukewarm attitudes to Nazi events reported by authorities. Fear naturally played some role in enforcing outward conformity, but less than it had during the Nazis' initial seizure of power. Nervousness and apprehension had faded for some as well. Indeed, open complaints and lacklustre event attendance suggest Germans may have been less afraid of their consequences.

To the extent such generalizations are possible, the Third Reich, and Hitler himself, were genuinely popular among Germans whose lives were improving, which was the case for the majority. Material advances did most to ensure satisfaction, but there was also widespread acclaim for the regime's remarkable successes. The response to remilitarizing the Rhineland was overwhelmingly positive, once it was clear Britain and France would not retaliate. Young people were especially ecstatic. Even German workers applauded: 'It's our country, after all,' one declared; 'Why shouldn't we be allowed to have any military there?'⁹ The predominantly Catholic Rhinelanders welcomed incoming German troops with flowers, cheers and euphoric choruses of 'Heil Hitlers', while Catholic bishops penned letters of gratitude to the *Führer*. Germany's dramatic staging of the summer Olympics in Berlin, in combination with its impressive medal count, brought another kind of restoration of international standing. That enhanced reputation on the world stage also fostered support for the regime at home.

Supporters shared many of the Nazis' ideas around German culture, especially their dislike of radically modernist art; however, this did not mean embracing only portraits of Stormtroopers, political speeches

Figure 2.2 A young girl greets a *Wehrmacht* soldier in Cologne (Rhineland), 7 March 1936 (Bettmann via Getty Images).

on the radio and films about the Nuremberg Rallies. Instead, they enjoyed entertaining movies, radio plays, concerts and novels that were not overtly propagandistic, since Goebbels had learned quickly that the drum must be kept in reserve to beat home a more effective message. There was also general support for – or at least widespread tolerance of – the regime's policies against political, social and racial outsiders, particularly since the phase of violent excesses seemed to be over. Broadly speaking, lower- and middle-class Protestants remained fully committed to the Third Reich, as were younger people overall; working-class and Catholic support was less consistent.

In early 1936, discontent among workers over rising food costs and shortages was widespread. The so-called fats crisis sparked workplace strikes and an uptick in reported communist sentiments and so-called malicious criticism of the regime. Though the Rhineland victory galvanized many workers' belief in Hitler, it could not distract them entirely from everyday concerns. Thus, the most significant factor in binding German workers to the Third Reich was the almost total elimination of unemployment by summer 1936. This created genuine enthusiasm for the regime's accomplishments and faith in its vision for Germany's future. By April 1937, SOPADE was acknowledging extensive support for the Nazi regime 'particularly in the working class'.[10] Authorities also noted how Germans regularly credited finding employment to Hitler himself, further inflating the 'Hitler Myth'.

As members of the racially privileged in-group, German workers benefitted in other ways that allowed a more enjoyable, comfortable life, including the consumption of pleasure in new forms. The Strength through Joy programme, for example, offered state-subsidized vacation packages. Although working-class participants were usually underrepresented on the holiday trains to the Black Forest, the Alps and the North Sea, in 1937, more took a trip than ever before. Purchases of 'People's' products, such as cheaper radios and refrigerators, increased. Even if dreams of driving a 'People's Car' (*Volkswagen*) went unfulfilled, automobile ownership was at least on the horizon of possibilities.

Not all workers were equal in Nazi Germany, and the armaments boom itself produced disparities. Those in preferred war-related industries (weapons, chemicals, steel, synthetics, shipyard and aircraft construction, etc.) experienced unparalleled prosperity in terms of wages, job security and promotion prospects, while those in other industries benefitted far less. Even in rearmament-related sectors, some grievances persisted through 1937. Wage freezes, long work hours and the intense work pace brought conflict directly to the factory floor. The German Labour Front representatives reported heckling during speeches. Strikes did erupt. Such openly defiant actions, rather than representing real opposition to Nazi Germany, suggest workers, at least in some industries, had gained newfound confidence to make demands of it. Their position of relative strength, with their labour in demand, meant the Nazi authorities and employers had to negotiate and acquiesce on occasion. The threat of terror still loomed – the *Gestapo* or other police units always arrived within hours of any strike, for example – but industrial workers' bargaining power, as individuals, had undeniably increased. They used it, in the main, to secure better working conditions and material security for themselves and their families. Working-class discontent, though perhaps 'never far from the surface' as historians have observed, never did surface in ways that might truly challenge the regime.[11]

Work in particular industries became so lucrative that it exacerbated the problem of what was called the 'flight from the land'. As peasants fled to find jobs elsewhere, labour shortages threatened to erode farmers' morale. Assistance from *Wehrmacht* soldiers and male and female Reich Labour Service recruits (all German men aged eighteen to twenty-five had to serve a six-month stint in the Service from 1935, but it was still voluntary for women at this stage) – often middle-class Germans unused to agricultural labour – was not enough at harvest time. Farmers' wives were especially overburdened. They and their husbands aired grievances surprisingly openly. By 1937, the proportion of farmers with Nazi Party membership had declined. However, young people who remained in their villages were more likely to support the Third Reich, having been exposed to Nazi propaganda in school and other youth organizations. Some hoped for careers as agricultural advisors and administrators within the regime. Despite irritation at Nazi meddling in church affairs, conservative farmers, Protestant and Catholic alike, welcomed the ongoing suppression of communism and applauded Germany's success on the world stage. SOPADE's September 1937 assessment summed this up neatly: peasant discontent was 'without great political significance'.[12]

Middle-class urban Germans also grumbled, while at the same time enjoying higher levels of prosperity. Civil service salaries, at least in certain sectors, finally rose after years of Depression-induced austerity. Those who were already connected to various Party organizations started to climb the ranks, not only in traditional sectors, but also in specifically Nazi institutions, like the *Gestapo*. An entirely new breed of white-collar bureaucrat appeared in the Third Reich to serve the racial state apparatus. The rewards were higher incomes, enhanced social mobility and status, and real power over the lives of others. For example, organizations like the Reich Genealogical Authority employed thousands to define 'Germanness'. One task involved researching and issuing the Ancestral Proof necessary to join the Nazi Party, wed, gain certain jobs, enter the military and more.

While not empowered to define German art and culture, artists in the Third Reich attempted to work towards the ideals trumpeted by Hitler. These very different 'workers' were increasingly crucial as the Nazis shifted attention in these years from the negative – purging racial and political outsiders and their 'degenerate' works – to the positive: creating a wholly 'German' aesthetics. The vast majority of the best-known, non-Jewish cultural figures in all fields had remained in Germany after 1933. Few joined the Nazi Party. Some, especially writers, embarked on a path of non-conformity and 'inner emigration', turning away from Nazi beliefs. Many more accommodated themselves very comfortably to what was now expected of them. This included Arno Breker, whose gigantic sculptures of 'Aryan' supermen went on display at the Great German Art Exhibitions from 1937, and director Leni Riefenstahl's filmed tributes to the Nazi Party Rallies. Others produced what Goebbels termed cheerful diversions: entertainment films, classical music concerts and romance novels with nary a swastika to be seen. Reliable artists experienced a real boost in prestige, working conditions and financial security in Nazi Germany.

This was a period of relative calm and increasing prosperity for most female members of the privileged people's community. Like men, more women were working again. The Nazis lifted the official – but regularly breached – prohibition on 'double earners' in 1937, and actively recruited women in certain sectors. The rearmament drive would soon mean a considerable increase in women in industry. Middle-class housewives enjoyed higher household incomes due to rising male employment. The Nazis' charity drives, like the annual Winter Relief programme, assisted some families who struggled despite full employment. At the same time, the Four Year Plan had adverse effects on women's day-to-day lives in the drive to national self-sufficiency. They bore the brunt of shortages, increased domestic labour and constant exhortations, demands and threats to do more with less. Nazi women's organizations targeted married women, who made the majority of household purchases, with an enormous tide of educational efforts. Exhibitions, slideshows, lectures, cinema newsreels, radio programmes and even board games repeated the same messages about saving, cooking, mending and spending. In 1937, housewifery became a formal part of the school curriculum for girls. Women had to 'shop German', which meant not only avoiding stores owned by Jews but also buying home-grown produce like apples rather than exotic bananas.

In reality, the regime-sponsored cooking classes and courses on childcare were often poorly attended, and some women found the educational films simplistic and patronizing. There was a near-constant stream of grumbling and jokes about shortages of items, like pork, and the shoddy quality of some substitute products, like cloth made of wood fibre that disintegrated upon laundering. Women also hoarded certain products when they became available, contrary to authorities' warnings. Yet at least some women felt their scrimping and saving were indeed contributing to the nation, validating their sacrifices and making them easier to bear.

Other obligations of Nazism could elicit decidedly positive reactions, especially among younger women. This period saw increasing pressure to 'volunteer' for the Reich Labour Service or to serve out a Duty Year doing agricultural labour or domestic service after high school. Neither were yet mandatory for all women, but thousands heeded the call nonetheless; at the end of 1937, the number of women in the Labour Service was double the 1935 level.[13] Some had joined under duress but more stepped up willingly. For every homesick, middle-class girl who chafed at hard physical labour, unwelcoming farmwives or communal life in barracks-style accommodation, many more, it appears, appreciated time spent in service to the nation. There were new friendships, opportunities for leadership roles, freedom from the familial environment and different parts of the Fatherland to see. In fact, some women describe this as one of the happiest and most influential phases of their lives. Meeting other Germans from lower-middle-class and working-class backgrounds was transformative for many middle-class young women. They recounted the deeply felt pleasure of embodying the *Volksgemeinschaft* in miniature.

Women also responded enthusiastically to traditional types of maternal care projects, like the Mother's Homes organized by the Nazi Welfare Organization. Usually located in the countryside, these offered rest, recuperation, fresh air, good food and support to women who could not afford it for themselves. They came with a large serving of Nazi ideology, but women's positive impressions were certainly not all coerced. For some, their stay was 'the most beautiful hours of our lives', all, they acknowledged, thanks to the *Führer*.[14]

The regime hoped such programmes would increase the birth rate, a necessity for national survival in the future; in the present, Germany's soldiers were more important. By 1937, the experience of being a soldier – if still only in peacetime – had become widely shared among young, male, insider Germans. Approximately 300,000 men, aged eighteen to forty-five, fulfilled their mandatory military service annually, either for a period of two years as full-time soldiers, or, for older men, two to three months per year followed by attachment to a reserve division. From a force of 100,000 men capped by the Treaty of Versailles, the German *Wehrmacht* had grown to almost 600,000 in thirty-six divisions by the end of 1937, the bulk of them infantry.[15] It was impossible, without serious repercussions, to refuse to serve. Even so, almost double the number of recruits enlisted voluntarily than were drafted, usually to find employment or escape a six-month stint in the Reich Labour Service. Under enormous pressure to expand, the German armed forces absorbed recruits from ever-wider walks of life, though the offer corps remained largely the preserve of men from upper-middle-class or even aristocratic backgrounds, who had attained the necessary secondary school qualifications.

German men of this generation had grown up in classrooms that glorified the soldierly experience and Great War heroes. By the time they enlisted, an increasing percentage of soldiers had continuous experience in other Nazi organizations, like the HJ, which instilled military values and provided physical training, including shooting practice, drilling and outdoor survival. Even without prior experience in a Nazi organization, many recruits knew something of a regimented, communal life from living in barracks in *Autobahn* work camps, for example. While the strict discipline, often dehumanizing cruelty of superiors and physical expectations of basic training were an unwelcome shock for some new soldiers, the benefits of plentiful food and adequate, if austere, accommodation were compensation for others, as was the excitement of large-scale manoeuvers, driving tanks and firing live ammunition. In any case, supporters rarely questioned the necessity of their service. Their pride and honour grew with the military's victory in the Rhineland and a larger public presence in German society. The *Wehrmacht* played a role in all major Nazi events, from the annual Party Rallies to the Olympics. While their *Führer* preached peace, these soldiers prepared for war. Intensive ideological indoctrination, aimed at a thoroughly Nazified military, helped harden them to that possibility. Propaganda and education also reinforced their real-world experiences of an apparently realized *Volksgemeinschaft*, at least for the rank and file. One new recruit recalled meeting his fellow soldiers, among them, an assembly line worker in a factory, a farm boy, the son of a schoolmaster and a 'city urchin'.[16] Many men genuinely valued communal experiences of being 'all the same in our service for the people', as a 1937 diary entry recorded.[17]

The largest, still-to-be coordinated institution not yet fully serving the Nazi state was the Catholic Church, which, from the Nazis' perspective, threatened the cohesion of the national community and blocked their totalitarian ambitions. Friction intensified throughout this period, with Catholic Germans openly protesting perceived violations of the Concordat, the agreement between Nazi Germany and the Vatican, as well as eugenic policies against the disabled. Catholic loyalty to Church fathers over the *Führer* endured, despite the Nazis' barrage of anticlerical propaganda making lurid accusations about sexual immorality, Jewish influence and communist corruption. Outraged, the regime turned to increasingly radical repressive measures to break bonds between the clergy and their flocks for good, including a series of sensationalist 'immorality trials' in 1936. Hundreds of Catholic clergy members stood trial for homosexuality, sexual misconduct and sexual abuse of minors; a large percentage of these alleged culprits had prior histories of opposition to the Nazi Party.

To the Nazis' chagrin, the trials and other forms of harassment and intimidation failed to divide Catholic communities or diminish the clergy's spiritual and even secular authority, especially in close-knit, predominantly Catholic small towns and villages. Because Catholics were too numerous, too influential and ultimately too racially valuable to alienate completely, the Nazis sometimes had to compromise. This does not mean, however, that German Catholics, angered as they were by the Nazis' threats, viewed themselves as anything other than true patriots and obedient citizens. Church leaders wanted to improve relations; neither they nor the laity opposed the Third Reich in principle. They willingly compartmentalized their grievances for fear of being cast as real outsiders – enemies of the Reich – themselves.

Attitudes to outsiders, and to their persecution, were ambiguous, diverse and contradictory among 'ordinary' insiders during all phases of the Third Reich. These years were no exception. Horror and outrage coexisted with genuine compassion, enthusiasm and calls for more radical actions. Knowledge of, and thus collective reactions to, Nazi persecution also changed over time. In 1936 and 1937, both were markedly different from what they had been and were later to be.

Supporters were much less likely to witness Nazi terror first-hand in these years. Arrests of political opponents were now sporadic, their numbers smaller, with less open violence. Sterilizations were ongoing, but took place out of sight. The Olympics paused some of the most heinous assaults on Jews. 'Aryanization' was largely invisible, apart from a name change on a store sign. At the same time, the concentration camps themselves largely vanished as topics of curiosity, conversation and concern according to evidence reproduced in the most recent studies. Fear alone does not explain it. Several other things do. First, on the most basic level, there were now far fewer camps – Himmler had closed hundreds – and far fewer inmates incarcerated in them. From a peak of 100,000 in 1933, there were approximately 4,000 in early 1936.[18] This meant fewer Germans actually knew anyone in a camp or lived in close proximity to one. Second, although Nazi propaganda about the camps had hardly been a reliable source about their real conditions, publicity about them had greatly diminished. Their deterrent value was no longer as important with the Third Reich on such solid foundations. The camps had become normalized: they were old news.

In the eyes of many, they were also 'normal', legitimate penal institutions since they increasingly imprisoned people many felt needed punishment, such as 'Gypsies', 'asocials' and 'habitual criminals', especially as it occurred out of sight. When unease arose, it was regularly only among those who lived nearby or had direct ties to the camps. Dachau, Sachsenhausen and Buchenwald edged towns and villages, and could not exist without a dense network of economic, infrastructural and social links to local populations. Camps needed electricity, water, gas, postal service, food delivery and transportation networks; their inmates laboured beyond the camp walls, visible to neighbours. Witnessing violence, deprivations or physical ill health first-hand could certainly lead to questions about conditions, but, as one historian recently writes, 'the dominant German "opinion" on the camps by this juncture was an impotent acceptance laced with indifference'.[19]

Only a minority of outsiders ended up in concentration camps, and in this period, relatively few Jewish Germans did. What then of supporters' attitudes to anti-Jewish persecution more generally? Ironically, the best assessment comes from Nazi sources themselves, which often commented on the population's very diverse mood regarding the 'Jewish Question'. An episode at a Christmas market in one small town typified the range of responses. Outside a Jewish-owned store, a large crowd gathered, probably instigated by Party functionaries, who reported, 'Some of the people were hostile towards the Jewish shop, while others simply stood there, indifferent. A few people also made remarks favourable to the Jews. ... [Others] chanted "Death to Judas".[20] Despite this diversity, there was undoubtedly a normalizing of antisemitism in 1936 to 1937. Years of antisemitic propaganda and institutionalized racism had an effect. While most insiders were not fanatical Jew-haters, they gladly profited from 'Aryanization' opportunities, like purchasing real estate from Jewish owners forced to sell at cut-rate prices, while also continuing commercial dealings with Jews when it served their economic interests.

Informing on other Germans or denouncing outsiders was generally driven by personal rather than immediate political motivations. Denunciations thus tell us less about public levels of support for Nazi racial policies than might first appear. They do tell us that Germans expected the Nazi regime to deal, in some way, with outsiders and unwelcome social behaviours. That the Nazis were successful in meeting such expectations explains in part why these years were later seen as the 'good old days' under Hitler. Whatever their responses to Nazi racism, many Germans likely concurred with one man's post-war justification for supporting the Third Reich overall: 'The fact that things were getting better with Adolf's help ... pleased us. It's as simple as that.'[21] Unstated was that better for 'us' meant horrifying for 'them'.

Racial and social outsiders

Those who fell outside the *Volksgemeinschaft* had widely varying experiences across 1936 and 1937. Nazi persecution changed little for some; for others it escalated; for still others it began for the first time. In some ways, these were quieter and more predictable years for Jewish Germans than the first ones of Nazi rule. Antisemitic violence on the streets largely disappeared. Certain Jewish-owned businesses, buoyed by national economic recovery, even recorded improved fortunes.

During the Olympic year, there was a brief, superficial hiatus from official antisemitic propaganda and more overt forms of harassment. Yet although there was also a pause in anti-Jewish legislation of national scope after the Nuremberg Laws, measures were extended at the regional and local levels that could have profound impacts on daily life. Overall, economic discrimination brought extremely harmful consequences.

In many places, Jews could hardly enter shops, let alone be successful shopkeepers. A spate of new policies – like the ban on 'Aryan' civil servants patronizing Jewish doctors, pharmacists, hospitals and nursing homes – further solidified their outsider status and negatively impacted their livelihoods. No national decree demanded that Jewish Germans be dismissed from private enterprises, but as employers voluntarily coordinated their labour forces in line with Nazi prejudice, more lost their jobs. Pressures to 'Aryanize' Jewish-owned properties and businesses, usually at a major loss to their owners, intensified. By the end of 1937, 60 per cent of small-scale Jewish proprietors were out of business, including over 80 per cent of retail establishments.[22] In the face of widespread poverty, Jewish mutual aid organizations lamented not being able to help all the individuals and families seeking assistance.

Jewish emigration numbers, which had risen in 1936 after the imposition of the Nuremberg Laws, actually decreased in 1937. The decrease was fuelled less by newfound beliefs that a secure future in Germany was possible than by the economic penalties the regime imposed to dispossess the Jews. These included increased restrictions on how much foreign currency emigrants could take out of the country and the Reich Flight Tax, a Weimar-era law, which demanded 25 per cent of emigrants' assets. Departing therefore meant impoverishment for most Jewish Germans, who, were they lucky enough to find a country to take them, had to give up the vast majority of their property. Fleeing now clearly meant for the duration of the Third Reich, shown by the intensified persecution of emigrants who dared to return to Germany. Subject to 're-education' in concentration or work camps, their release only came with proof of an imminent departure, this time for good. Patriotic Jewish Germans who stayed felt conflicting loyalties despite the ongoing persecution. Individual Great War veterans applauded the Rhineland remilitarization, and some younger Jews found it impossible to remain immune from the Olympic fever that gripped the country that year. Nevertheless, fear that things might get worse after the closing ceremonies was common.

For Jews held in concentration camps, it was hard to imagine anything worse. Only a tiny fraction of the Jewish German population had yet shared those experiences; by the mid-1930s, there were only a few dozen at each of the major camps. Their situation deteriorated immediately after the Olympic guests left. Himmler now had to approve the release of every Jewish prisoner. In February 1937, the Nazis designated Dachau as the central camp for Jews, although they were also interned at the major new camps of Sachsenhausen and Buchenwald. There were separate Jewish barracks, and Jewish prisoners had to wear a yellow triangle to mark their race alongside a triangle identifying their 'crime'; worn together they formed a Star of David. Segregation allowed SS guards to perpetrate collective abuses on Jewish inmates, including the hardest labour, most disgusting tasks and worst verbal and physical cruelties. The number of Jewish camp prisoners remained comparatively small in this period, and most could still expect release. Yet as the number grew, so too did trepidation about what lay over the horizon, not only for those in the camps but also for the Jewish community at large.

The Nazis sterilized more Germans before this period than during it, but the operations continued and the physical and psychological effects on victims endured. Many experienced lingering pain; others died, having failed to recover from the operation. Sterilization by X-ray, introduced more frequently from 1936, posed other long-term consequences. Not surprisingly, victims were denied medical benefits by health insurance offices. Banned from 'normal' schools, sterilized Germans had to abandon career plans. One woman recalled having to give up her dream of being a kindergarten teacher after her 1937 operation.[23] Some Germans committed suicide as the awareness of the loss of their fertility deepened or dawned for the first time.

Just as being deemed 'hereditarily ill' was always very dangerous in the Third Reich, so too was the label 'asocial'. As time passed, there were more ways for Germans to deviate from Nazi norms, such as failing to donate to Party charity drives or send children to the Hitler Youth. The regime rarely punished a single offense in these years if committed by otherwise good 'Aryans'. By contrast, designated 'asocial' Germans, wearing black triangle badges, filled the camps in greater numbers, especially from December 1937 when the regime introduced new legislation authorizing further grounds for their incarceration.

The Sinti and Roma peoples, then usually referred to as 'Gypsies', first arrived in Germany from the Indian subcontinent in the fifteenth century. Numbering approximately 30,000 in this period, their largely itinerant lifestyle, dress, customs and lack of traditional employment had made them outsiders for centuries. Viewed as thieves and their settlements as public nuisances, they experienced heightened surveillance, discrimination and exclusion in the Weimar Republic. The Nazis escalated those practices; as 'asocials' and 'habitual criminals', they were sterilized and confined indefinitely in prisons and concentration camps. As 'non-Aryans', Sinti and Roma Germans also fell under the Nuremberg Laws. While not a chief ideological obsession for Hitler – he never spoke of them in public, for example – 'Gypsies' were one of Himmler's preoccupations. In June 1936, in advance of the Summer Olympics, local police forces in major cities carried out raids and arrests, and searched the homes of 'Gypsy' families. They worked off information collected by the recently founded Reich Central Office for Suppressing the Gypsy Menace. Police officers placed some Sinti and Roma children in youth homes, then supervised construction of, and guarded, so-called gypsy camps. The largest of these, the euphemistically termed 'Rest Stop' Marzahn on the outskirts of Berlin, bordered a large sewage facility and a cemetery, a taboo location for Sinti and Roma. In July 1936, approximately 600 Sinti and Roma Germans were forcibly relocated to the encampment. Nine-year-old Otto Rosenberg was one of them, uprooted from the life he knew, where 'everybody knew everybody', to one behind barbed wire.[24]

Conditions in Marzahn were deplorable. There were only three water taps and two toilets. The lack of adequate hygiene led to quickly spreading infectious diseases. Women were only allowed to

Figure 2.3 A Sinti and Roma woman and two children look out a caravan window in the Marzahn 'Gypsy Camp' in a photograph taken by 'racial scientists' (Bundesarchiv, Bild 146-1987-035-17A).

leave to buy food. Men became forced labourers. Internees also had to submit to invasive physical examinations by racial 'researchers' dispatched by the national Centre for Racial Hygiene and Heredity Research. The Centre, led by the psychiatrist Dr Robert Ritter, quickly became the leading authority on the 'Gypsy problem'. Escape from Marzahn meant immediate transfer to one of the main concentration camps. As the Nazis' policies converged with, and legitimized, long-standing popular hostility towards 'Gypsies', life under Hitler became increasingly difficult for Sinti and Roma Germans.

Black Germans – an estimated 20,000 – were also victims of Nazi racism in these years. They included Africans from Germany's former colonies and their biracial offspring, as well as the much-maligned 'Rhineland bastards': the estimated 600–800 children of Black French and Belgian colonial soldiers (Rhineland occupiers after the First World War) and 'Aryan' mothers. Although defined as 'non-Aryans' under the Nuremberg Laws, these Black Germans were seen by the Nazis as a less significant threat than other racial outsiders given their small number and dispersal throughout the country. Their persecution was therefore more uneven and less coordinated, but no less painful, especially for individuals who had grown up in Germany, spoke perfect German, and bore German names. Hans-Jürgen Massaquoi, a Hamburg-born boy with a Liberian father, could not understand being barred from the Hitler Youth. 'My mother says I'm German just like anybody else,' he protested, while proudly wearing a swastika pin on his sweater.[25]

Black Germans found it difficult to find employment and housing in Nazi Germany, while also being ineligible for most welfare schemes. Emboldened by state-sanctioned racism, everyday harassment and intimidation from other Germans were common. By 1936, Black Germans were no longer welcome at public schools in some locations. Localized bans prohibited their access to parks, playgrounds and swimming pools. In 1936, the regime decided to sterilize the 'Rhineland bastards' based on research by German scientists that revealed their supposedly inferior physical and intellectual abilities. These operations were to be done in secret since the existing legislation made no formal provision for sterilizing 'non-Aryans', only the disabled and 'asocial'. German doctors examined the children, aged seven to seventeen, and submitted their reports. *Gestapo* agents often took them by force to the hospitals. Some 400 Black German children were sterilized.[26]

The victimization of male German homosexuals also escalated in this period. In October 1936, Himmler created the Reich Central Office for Combatting Homosexuality and Abortion, thereby linking two 'crimes' affecting birth rates within the *Volk*. Its primary task was compiling a card index of all known – suspected or convicted –

homosexuals in the country, accompanied by fingerprints and photographs wherever possible. The list had 42,000 names within four years.[27] Local police authorities were to report all suspected homosexual activity, especially cases involving young people, soldiers and clergymen, as well as male prostitutes. Relying heavily on denunciations, the police raided homes and meeting places, seized address books and used undercover agents to identify suspects. Most gay victims were working-class. Without private apartments and homes, they met with partners in public places, making them more vulnerable to arrest.

The December 1937 Decree against Dangerous Habitual Criminals put men with multiple charges of homosexuality in even greater danger. They were frequently sent to concentration camps after serving their judicial sentences in 'regular' German prisons. Within the camps, the pink triangle prisoners faced brutal physical and sexual abuse at the hands of guards and even other inmates. Most fellow prisoners shunned them, fearing being labelled homosexual as well. Especially isolated and powerless, their suicide rate was higher than that of any other prisoner group. Hundreds of gay men agreed to castration to secure their release from prisons or camps; others were forced to undergo the procedure.

As the experience of gay men in the camps shows, persecution did not necessarily bond outsiders to one another in the Third Reich. Even among the Nazis' victims, antisemitism and homophobia were common, sterilizing the 'diseased' and disciplining the 'asocial' met with some approval, and hostility to 'Gypsies' and prejudice based on skin colour were widely shared. Such sentiments separated victim groups from one another and hindered collective action by outsiders to resist Nazi oppression.

Resisters

Significant, fundamental resistance to the Third Reich was at its lowest point in this period. There were no movements or actions that seriously endangered the Nazis' hold on power and far fewer arrests for treasonable offenses. However, there were undercurrents of opposition. Not surprisingly, these arose among those most threatened by Nazi ideology, as they had since 1933, but they also now emerged from previously unexpected sources.

By 1937, the vast majority of communist and socialist resisters were 'exiled, imprisoned, or dead'.[28] Mass *Gestapo* arrests took care of those small, isolated groups, like the Socialist Front in Hannover, which had continued printing and distributing leaflets, liaising with supporters abroad and carrying out minor sabotage efforts. Political opponents sent to concentration camps had to wear red triangles on their prisoners' uniforms. The longer Hitler was in power, the harsher People's Court verdicts against 'traitors' also became. As death sentences increased, leftist despair grew. Former trade union activists watched as ongoing labour conflicts, contrary to their expectations, failed to transform into overt political opposition or even lessen workers' support, however passive, for Hitler. For some Germans, there remained only one other way to fight fascism: enlisting in the International Brigades against Francisco Franco's Nationalist forces in the Spanish Civil War. Most of these men had already fled Germany before journeying to Spain but a few departed only now. Two thousand Germans, the vast majority of them communists, died in Spain trying to stop what they had failed to prevent in their own country. Franco's eventual victory in 1939 was yet another blow to the German left.

On the opposite side of the political spectrum, unease was brewing. Some conservative circles, once enthusiastic about the Third Reich, now began to coalesce around a shared desire for Germany's return to the rule of law. They included men like Lieutenant Colonel Hans Oster, working within Germany's Military Intelligence Service (*Abwehr*) and Carl Goerdeler, Mayor of Leipzig and Reich Price Commissioner. At odds with Goering over the Four Year Plan, Goerdeler was one of the few in his ranks to criticize the Nuremberg Laws. He resigned as Mayor in March 1937 when a Leipzig statue of Felix Mendelssohn-Bartholdy, a Jewish German composer, was demolished over his vocal objections. For him, the goal had become clear: Hitler must go. For now, however, only a tiny number of conservative elites agreed.

Christians continued to come into conflict with the Nazi regime. The Protestant 'Church Struggle' between Bishop Müller's 'German

Christians' and Confessing Church supporters blazed less fiercely, but an irrevocable split now opened up between moderate and radical Confessing Church members, the latter led by Martin Niemoeller. He had grown increasingly critical of the Nazis' ideological assault on the Christian faith. In June 1936, he addressed a memorandum to Hitler, which condemned the extreme elements of the Nazi racial world view. The *Gestapo* took Niemoeller into custody the following month. Niemoeller survived the Third Reich, but only after years spent in Sachsenhausen and Dachau, at times in solitary confinement. His detention triggered a crackdown in 1937 on Protestant pastors, especially the very few who dared to defend Jews and Judaism in their sermons. Despite parishioners' unease about these arrests, the vast majority of Protestant Germans retained not only their Christian faith but also their faith in Hitler to safeguard and defend the values they most cherished.

As we have seen, 1936 to 1937 marked the high point in tensions between the Catholic Church and the Nazi regime. The sterilization programme remained contentious, but vocal opposition to it had quieted. By contrast, anger at the regime's perceived efforts to 'de-Christianize' the nation inspired noisy, open defiance and protest, as in November 1936, when the Nazi Governor of the state of Oldenburg announced a ban on crucifixes (and portraits of Marin Luther) in public places and schools. Catholic priests denounced the decree from the pulpit. Parishioners sent a flood of letters and petitions against it. One town erected a large cross on its church tower and illuminated it with spotlights. The Governor rescinded the order, a rare, dramatic – and short-lived – victory for Catholics, but this was a relatively minor issue on which the Nazis could afford to relent. Later protests, against the closure of Catholic schools for example, were met with arrests. Even as they continued to fight interference in religious matters, most German Catholics refrained from outright conflict with the Nazi state. 'There is a time', Cardinal Michael von Faulhaber observed, 'to be silent'.[29] The Catholic Church generally remained silent about the regime's antisemitism as it had since 1933. Pope Pius's March 1937 encyclical (a letter to his Bishops), entitled 'With Burning Concern', was an exception. While largely focused on perceived violations of the Concordat, the encyclical did say that exalting one race above others, as Nazi ideology did, was incompatible with Christianity. Yet the Pope condemned neither the National Socialist regime as a whole nor Hitler himself.

Unlike Protestants and Catholics who emphasized their overall loyalty to the state, Jehovah's Witnesses, a minority Christian sect numbering 20,000, explicitly rejected allegiance to a secular authority. They refused to give the Hitler salute, allow their children to join the HJ and BDM, fly the swastika flag or participate in mass celebrations on occasions like Hitler's birthday. They also actively proselytized, usually through doorstep conversations and leaving literature in mailboxes. In consequence, Nazi authorities disbanded their meetings, dissolved their Watchtower Society and confiscated their publications. They removed Witness children from their homes and placed them in reform schools. The *Gestapo* also worked on creating a registry of all known Witnesses. The introduction of mandatory military conscription further escalated the conflict, since Witness beliefs prohibited fighting for a worldly power. Arrests for draft dodging increased dramatically by 1937 and the number of camp inmates wearing purple triangles, the badges forced on Jehovah's Witnesses, grew. In June 1937, Witnesses distributed almost 70,000 copies of an 'open letter' to homes across Germany and to government officials, calling attention to the harassment and violence they had suffered. Mass arrests followed, with some 6,000 Witnesses taken into custody over the Third Reich's lifespan.[30] At any time, the Jehovah's Witnesses could have gained freedom from persecution by renouncing their faith; almost all steadfastly refused.

German children and teenagers were generally enthusiastic Hitler supporters and by early 1936, nearly two-thirds of those aged ten to eighteen belonged to the Hitler Youth.[31] However, young Catholics generally preferred their own, still-permitted groups, and working-class youth generally stayed away from the HJ. The Nazis found this situation intolerable; the Hitler Youth became the only lawful German youth organization in December 1936. This intensified coordination of youth spurred greater nonconformity, unrest and even active opposition. Without other options for collective activity, what had previously been new and exciting grew more burdensome. The more 'normal' it became to attend, and the more obligatory meetings and events filled their calendars, the less some young Germans attended. Absenteeism became a problem.

The regime found the persistence of 'club-like' organizations more worrying. These anti-militarist leftovers from Weimar's independent youth movement, like the German Boys Club of November 1 and the Neroth Hikers, persisted in secret. In response, Himmler ordered the *Gestapo* to establish a special office to root out these 'club-like' activities. The existence of so-called wild youth gangs or cliques caused the Nazis acute anxiety. The phenomenon took root in industrialized districts of the Rhineland-Ruhr and working-class suburbs of major cities. Some gangs, like the Kittelsbach Pirates in Düsseldorf or the Leipzig Hound Packs, were broadly sympathetic to communism; others were more motley collections of youngsters disgruntled with HJ uniforms, routine and discipline. Exceedingly few of their members actively opposed the Third Reich itself. As one recalled, 'The main problem was not that we were against the Nazis but that the Nazis were against us.'[32] They were indeed. In autumn 1937, for example, the Cologne People's Court sentenced boys in the Navajos gang to stints in harsh work camps and youth detention centres. These children, more youthful rebels than committed opponents, still threatened the homogeneity of the *Volksgemeinschaft*. The longer the Nazi regime was in power, the more ruthlessly it pursued them.

Active resistance by the racially persecuted was even more dangerous, but they pursued it nonetheless. Nearly one in ten young adults arrested for treason or high treason had some Jewish ancestry.[33] While individuals like Herbert and Marianne Baum continued their brave anti-fascist leaflet campaign, Jewish Germans more commonly resisted oppression in personal and private, not political, ways. Thousands sent petitions to police precincts or the courts, pleading for leniency for themselves or on behalf of others, or challenging the latest antisemitic actions and restrictions. They were sometimes successful, if not in their ultimate aim then because the authorities took them seriously enough to allocate resources to deal with them and involved other agencies to make their decisions, sapping time,

Figure 2.4 The Navajos youth gang in Cologne in 1936 or 1937 (Courtesy of NS-Documentation Center of the City of Cologne).

energy and personnel power. Other protests, while still personal, were not at all private. They included all kinds of defiant acts, from defacing Nazi swastikas to defying bans on swimming in public pools or attending the cinema.

As they had since 1933, Germany's Jewish communities worked cooperatively to sustain one another. They focused largely on the younger generations, such as increasing youth retraining programmes for bettering emigration chances. The Jewish Culture League also continued its efforts in this period. Little of what it produced, presented and published said much about the current moment, but there were exceptions, which alluded to Nazi persecution. One chillingly prescient 1936 poem bravely expressed the fear that 'one day we will fall like birds struck down by the lethal bullets of our prosecutors'.[34]

While sterilizations of disabled and 'asocial' Germans declined from their 1935 peak – increasingly the 'asocial', especially 'habitual criminals', were sent to concentration camps instead – the practice continued throughout 1936 and 1937. Sterilization candidates and their families thus kept up their attempts to stop the operation, whether in statements given at Hereditary Health Courts, personal appeals to authorities, enlisting support from Catholic clergy or simply not turning up for appointments. Some individuals fled their hometowns to hide with relatives, at least temporarily postponing the procedure. Some physically disabled Germans worked collectively to challenge their outsider status by differentiating themselves from 'useless eaters' (the mentally disabled) and dangers to the community (the 'asocial'). Groups such as the Reich Union of the Deaf and the Reich Association of the Blind sought to dispel misinformation about the hereditary nature of such disabilities and to portray their members as useful and productive members of the *Volk*. Rarely successful, such communal attempts to renegotiate identities under attack in the Third Reich were brave. However, by maintaining they were not burdens to the state, physically disabled Germans implied that other Germans were.

By 1936, the Nazis' persecution of Sinti and Roma, Black and homosexual Germans had escalated substantially. Given their small numbers, and their isolated and marginalized status, collective action was not an option for them. These Germans did not have equivalent bodies to the Reich Representation of the Jews in Germany or the Reich League of the Physically Handicapped dedicated to community self-defence against Nazi oppression. Moreover, as targets of widespread societal prejudices, they had fewer opportunities to cooperate with existing opposition cells, whether communist, conservative or Catholic. Instead, these outsiders undertook actions as individuals and families to resist the regime's intentions through the kind of 'bureaucratic defense' engaged in by other victims.[35] After round-ups and raids on 'Gypsies', a small number of Sinti and Roma Germans petitioned the authorities, urging the release of arrested loved ones. Some 'Aryan' mothers refused to sign paperwork consenting to the sterilization of their Black children, which appears to have prevented, or at least delayed, the operation on occasion. Gay men, however, ceased sending the kinds of protest letters they once had; actively drawing attention to themselves as victimized homosexuals was a dangerous strategy for it might lead to further police attention. Still, during court trials, gay men bravely challenged the enemy label, with some displaying their Great War medals to prove their patriotism. Such actions and others like them rarely achieved their aims, and if they did, only temporarily. Nonetheless, when those Germans who faced its greatest dangers dared in any way to contest the Nazi regime, they resisted the total realization of its goals.

CHAPTER 3
VICTORY AND PERSECUTION
(1938–1940)

Spectacular Nazi achievements and radically intensified persecution marked the years 1938 to 1940. On 12 March 1938, German troops under a new supreme commander of the *Wehrmacht* – Hitler himself – crossed the border into Austria. The following day, Austria was officially incorporated into what now became the Greater German Reich. On 1 October 1938, the Reich became even 'Greater' with the incorporation of the Sudetenland, formerly part of Czechoslovakia. British and French efforts to appease Hitler through such concessions proved futile. The *Wehrmacht* went on to invade the Czech provinces of Bohemia and Moravia in March 1939, turning them into a 'Reich Protectorate'.

Throughout 1938, the Nazi regime drastically increased antisemitic legislation in all areas under its control. On the evening of 9–10 November 1938, 'legal' measures erupted into open violence. Across the expanded Reich, SA, SS and HJ members, alongside 'ordinary' Germans, shattered the storefronts of Jewish businesses, burned synagogues and ransacked private homes in what became known as *Kristallnacht*: The Night of Broken Glass. They murdered well over 100 Jews. Approximately 30,000 Jewish men were interned in concentration camps. On 30 January 1939, the sixth anniversary of his assumption of power, Hitler openly threatened the 'annihilation of the Jewish race in Europe' in the event of another world war. The speech also announced, if in a more veiled fashion, his intentions for war.

That war began on 1 September 1939, when the *Wehrmacht* invaded Poland. Britain and France declared war on Nazi Germany two days later. A recently signed Non-Aggression Pact with the Soviet Union

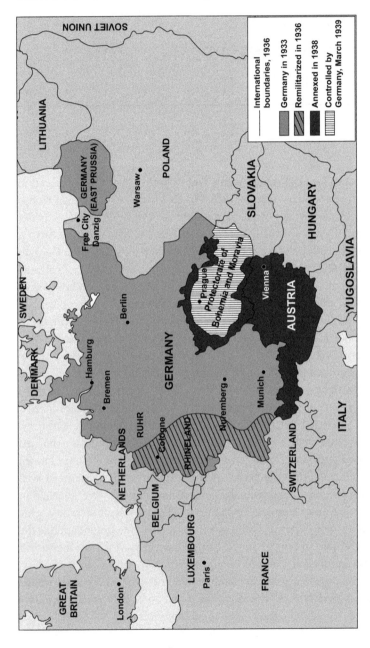

Map 2. Greater Germany in August 1939.

meant Hitler did not need to fear hostilities on two fronts. 'Lightning War' (*Blitzkrieg*) tactics – surprise rapid attacks by motorized infantry formations with airpower support – ensured a quick victory. Greater Germany annexed the western regions of Poland, while, to the East, an area called the General Government, which included Warsaw, came under its direct control. Himmler's SS supervised the building and sealing of Jewish ghettos across Poland. The city of Oświęcim, near Cracow, became the site of a new concentration and labour camp. The Germans called it Auschwitz.

Having successfully invaded Denmark and Norway in April 1940, Hitler turned on 10 May 1940 to Luxembourg, Belgium, the Netherlands and France. Within six weeks, Germany brought all of these countries under its control and began to exploit them economically to benefit the *Volk*, while millions of non-Germans suffered brutal Nazi aggression. At the same time, the Nazis' persecution of disabled and 'asocial' Germans turned lethal. The war's beginning saw Hitler authorize top-secret child and adult 'euthanasia' (i.e. killing) programmes. German doctors murdered children by drug injections and starvation in hospitals, and gassed adults with carbon monoxide in purpose-built gas chambers at six 'euthanasia' centres spread across the country. As Nazi Germany expanded its living space, its power over German lives also grew.

Nazis

For the Nazis, the German Reich becoming 'Greater' brought back the excitement of the movement's early years, its glorious 'period of struggle'. Expansion created new opportunities – for personal aggrandizement, ideological experimentation and national renewal – that had thus far remained out of reach. A glorious future seemed guaranteed, raising the Nazis' faith in the *Führer* to new heights. Hitler's decisions and actions determined events more than ever before, even as his regime continued to concern itself with popular opinion and respond to individual innovations on the ground. By the end of 1940, Hitler's power was close to its zenith. His internal position was secure and his authority effectively absolute. As one spectacular foreign policy success followed another, Hitler's belief that he had a divinely ordained mission deepened. His ambition to control the entire continent, and his conviction that war and expansion were critical to the survival of National Socialism itself, accelerated his timetable for military action.

With the fall of France, Hitler seemed to have rewritten history by reversing the outcome of the Great War. Heralded by his inner circle and many top generals as a military genius, his popularity soared within the general population. Respect and admiration created an echo chamber that reinforced Hitler's determination to lead without heeding anyone's advice, especially the old conservative elites. That had been dramatically symbolized by his purge in early 1938 of several top generals, including two at the very top: War Minister Werner von Blomberg and Werner von Fritsch, Commander-in-Chief of the Army. At that time, Hitler had dissolved the War Minister's office and taken over as Supreme Commander of the *Wehrmacht* himself. Yet the more control he took, the more his miscalculations as political leader and military commander had long-run consequences. Prominent among these was his assumption that France and Britain would do nothing when Germany invaded Poland. Britain's refusal even to consider peace after the fall of France in 1940 was totally unexpected and blocked Hitler's intended conclusion to the war in the West.

Preoccupied with foreign policy and military campaigns, Hitler grew even further removed from the daily running of the Reich. In any case, economic problems, labour crises and agricultural issues did not overly concern him since he believed further expansion would solve them all. Where Hitler did play a decisive role was in the persecution of racial outsiders, though always carefully distancing himself from violence perpetrated against them. The common refrain that 'the *Führer* knew nothing' about the worst crimes of these years shows how skilfully he masked his role in public. He let others intensify the persecution of Jewish Germans throughout 1938, staying in the background while fully approving. In Hitler's view, changed circumstances meant the timing was right for more severe anti-Jewish measures. The end to unemployment erased fears

Figure 3.1 The *Führer* greets crowds in Berlin during celebrations of the fall of France, July 1940 (©CORBIS/Corbis via Getty Images).

about the repercussions of closing down Jewish businesses. His total commitment to war and expansion made foreign opinion infinitely less concerning. Incorporating thousands of Austrian and Czech Jews had cancelled any 'progress' made through emigration. Hitler therefore gladly authorized the *Kristallnacht* pogrom on 9 November while allowing Joseph Goebbels to be the instigator.

That evening, Goebbels gave an incendiary speech to assembled Nazi functionaries in Munich, urging them to let the Jews feel the people's alleged anger. He even gave specific instructions about what supposedly spontaneous outbursts might look like. It was also Goebbels, who, once things began to spin out of control, ordered an end to the action while sharply intensifying antisemitic propaganda. The media in the newly incorporated territories, coordinated with the Reich Culture Chamber, peddled the same hate-filled antisemitism. Goebbels had little interest in actual military strategy, but his propaganda machine played a critical wartime role, celebrating military successes and demonizing the enemy, especially the British. German press and radio followed his guidelines, which were inspired by his fervent belief in the myths he peddled: Hitler was infallible and the Third Reich was invincible.

Kristallnacht: The Night of Broken Glass

On the evening of 9–10 November 1938, attacks on Jewish properties, synagogues, homes and bodies erupted across Greater Germany. The Nazis claimed these were acts of revenge for the recent murder of a minor German diplomat in Paris. Ernst vom Rath had been killed by seventeen-year-old Herschel Grynszpan, a Jew born in Germany, whose Polish parents had recently been deported. In reality, plans were already afoot for violent assaults on Jewish Germans and a final seizure of their assets; vom Rath's death was the necessary spark. *Kristallnacht* also provided the opportunity for the regime to proceed with the total 'de-Jewification' of the German economy and removing Jews' remaining freedoms.

Kristallnacht is the most common term in the North American context, but German scholars usually prefer the word pogrom, historically meaning violent riots by mobs against minorities. Since many Jewish communities themselves hold annual *Kristallnacht* commemorations, and the event certainly encompassed pogrom-like grassroots violence, this book uses both terms interchangeably.

Hitler's infamous prophecy of January 1939 about the annihilation of the Jews in the event of war reveals he was already imagining their physical destruction, even if the methods for it still had to be worked out. Though solving the 'Jewish Question' was secondary to military matters for Hitler through 1940, he had no doubt, as with any other difficulty, that war itself would provide the answer. Similarly, although he reluctantly reined in the Nazi assault on the Christian churches, recognizing its potential impact on morale, he foresaw a final reckoning after the war was won.

Not all could be postponed. The war immediately emboldened Hitler to authorize a solution to the 'problem' of physically disabled and mentally ill adults and children: their murder. The Nazis had considered a 'euthanasia' law since 1933. Exploiting a petition from the family of a severely disabled toddler requesting a so-called mercy death, Hitler charged his personal physician and the head of the Nazi Party's Chancellery of the *Führer* with implementing the programme. The *Führer's* Chancellery also led the top-secret adult 'euthanasia' programme (under the code name T4) meant to free the nation of 'useless eaters'. Fearing that a formal law might attract too much negative attention, Hitler chose instead to operate in secrecy. In October 1939, he issued a decree on his personal stationery authorizing certain physicians to kill 'incurable' patients. This was indeed an 'irreversible advance in the direction of genocide'.[1]

Hermann Goering's star briefly reached new heights in 1938 with his promotion to Field Marshal and designation as the *Führer's* nominal successor. Thereafter, his standing was eroded by the failure of the Air Force – over which he had complete control – to protect Germany from aerial attack. The Allied bombing of Berlin in late August 1940 punctured his boasts about the *Luftwaffe's* civil defence capabilities. Mass German bombing of English industrial and civilian targets (the Blitz) had just begun but the Battle of Britain, between German planes and those of the British Royal Air Force, was already lost. As Goering's standing in Hitler's eyes declined, he was increasingly shunted to the sidelines in foreign policy.

Although Goering had real concerns about the looming crisis in war production, he largely kept them to himself. While the limited resources of Germany's war economy could still fuel expansion, Goering's position as head of the Four Year Plan was unassailable; indeed, he gained an ever-wider scope of economic responsibilities, which he refused to delegate. His greatest success in this arena was in maximizing the regime's chokehold on Jewish Germans' economic lives to the *Volk's* benefit. He used new powers granted in winter 1938/1939 for private gain, too, confiscating Jewish-owned artworks for his personal collection. Outraged by *Kristallnacht* property damage, which destroyed assets ripe for 'Aryanization', his antisemitism was never in doubt. He preferred they had 'killed 200 Jews', he declared.[2] Indeed, Goering's renewed commitment to solving the 'Jewish Question' meant closer contacts between him and Heinrich Himmler's SS, although he believed a 'final solution' could come only after a final victory. The focus now was on expelling Jews from the economy and the theft of all they owned. Under Goering's loose supervision, the SS would determine what to do with them thereafter.

The enemy within remained an obsession for Reich Leader SS Himmler. Under his command, his protégé, Reinhard Heydrich, grew more powerful in 1939 with the consolidation of various security agencies into Berlin's Reich Security Main Office, thus facilitating terror against German outsiders more effectively. Heydrich's SS Security Service turned into an expansive intelligence superstructure, which protected national security by spying on Germans at home and abroad. He also headed the Reich Central Office for Jewish Emigration in Berlin, established by Goering in January 1939. By October, Adolf Eichmann, its director, was using every available means to dispossess Jewish Germans trying to leave, making their escape from the German Reich exceedingly difficult.

The war promised to fulfil Himmler's dreams of a European 'new order' with the SS as its masters. Conquered lands were to be 'cleansed' of their local populations and 'Germanized': resettled by ethnic Germans from the Baltics and Eastern Europe. The 'Jewish Question' naturally remained central, but for Himmler, the 'German Question' needed to be resolved first. According to his ten-year plan for making Germany Jew-free, deporting Jews from the Reich and the Protectorate to the General Government in Poland would have to wait. In the meantime, accelerating Jewish emigration remained official Nazi policy. Himmler also presided over uprooting hundreds of thousands of 'racially inferior' Poles from their homes to make way for Germans. With the prospect of conquering the Soviet Union in sight, Himmler, Heydrich and Eichmann began to imagine ever more radical, explicitly genocidal Jewish policy, with SS men in the vanguard, which now endangered Jewish Europeans across the entire continent.

The *Anschluss* and November pogrom of 1938 had already radicalized antisemitic persecution; however, with the invasion of Poland and the launch of the 'euthanasia' programme, SS men became systematic killers. As members of the SS Special Task Forces (*Einsatzgruppen*), they carried out mass executions of Polish non-combatants. As SS doctors, they murdered disabled adults and children. In all cases, they worked towards fulfilling what they understood Hitler's desires to be, and felt empowered to act even without clear directives. This intensified the process and set the stage for the more methodical targeting of their enemies, especially Jews, not only in the occupied territories but also at home. Later rewards – including higher status within the Nazi machinery of death – justified commanders' initiatives on the ground.

Their subordinates, from different age cohorts, social groups and regions, proved willing to act as killers. In only a short time, one Special Task Force member later wrote, 'We became as hard as steel.'[3] The elite combat troops of the Waffen SS, the SS military division founded in 1939, gained an especially fierce reputation as fanatical fighters alongside regular *Wehrmacht* units, torching Polish villages, murdering Jews and burning synagogues as they went. They saw action in the Netherlands and France as well. Himmler's SS also increasingly presided over working people to death in its growing economic empire, which came to depend on the mass exploitation of slave labour.

Even as the SS consolidated its control of security and racial policy, the SA remained a significant force in the Hitler state. Well over one million men donned the SA Brownshirt, the symbol of a commitment to defending core Nazi values. Most did so only part-time, combining service in the SA with other careers, unlike the professional, full-time Stormtroopers of earlier times. For longer-serving SA men, 1938 marked a return to the 'good old days' of 1933; once again, they could humiliate, threaten and beat up Jews with impunity with the occupations of Austria and the Sudetenland. SA terror targeted 'Gypsies' and Czechs here as well. During *Kristallnacht*, the Stormtroopers took a leading role as the core shock troops damaging property, and committing arson, looting and beatings. In this period, SA men provided the muscle for the numerous victory parades in Berlin, lining the streets to hold back ardent Hitler admirers. They played an important part in providing paramilitary training to German men through their various shooting organizations and riding clubs. They also fought for Hitler as *Wehrmacht* soldiers. In August and September 1939, almost one-third of the SA membership was drafted for military service. SA men too old or not sufficiently fit for the draft often found their wartime roles disappointing. These centred mostly on securing the home front: air alert duties, building bomb shelters, caring for the families of men at the front and transporting wounded soldiers. Some imagined a brighter future in Hitler's Europe after the war.

The Hitler Youth expanded exponentially in this period. Once membership became mandatory in March 1939, it became the largest youth organization in the world with 8.7 million members.[4] Its members played an integral role in *Kristallnacht* violence. HJ actions were both spontaneous in certain locations and steered from above in others. Older teenage boys predominated, but children of all ages threw stones at synagogue windows, chanted antisemitic slurs, cheered the crash of broken glass and looted stores and private homes. In Leipzig, Hitler Youths even attacked a Jewish nursing home. The children's participation was so excessively enthusiastic, and so difficult to stop once unleashed, the *Gestapo* reported widespread public condemnation of it. The war gave new purpose to young Nazis who were eager to do their bit. There were constant collection drives for scrap metal and bones for fertilizer. BDM girls knit scarves and sewed slippers for soldiers, or distributed provisions to departing troop trains.

The *Gauleiter* (Regional Leaders) of the Nazi Party hoped Greater Germany's victories might bring further personal gain. As a group, their importance grew, albeit with variations between the Old Reich and newly incorporated or occupied territories. The extensive powers enjoyed in the new regions were envied 'at home', but all *Gauleiter* shared a vital role in radicalizing antisemitism as the country expanded. For instance, it was to a group of three dozen *Gauleiter* – gathered on

9 November 1938 in Munich to commemorate the 1923 *putsch* – that Goebbels's speech, authorized by Hitler, gave the signal to orchestrate nation-wide Party violence against Jews across the Reich. After the war, several of these men claimed they had opposed Goebbels's directives, but while some may have proceeded less ruthlessly than others, there were no truly resistant *Gauleiter*. Moreover, Party leaders like themselves were first in line to benefit from the intensified seizures of Jewish businesses and assets that immediately followed.

By contrast, formal Party contributions to the war effort were relatively insignificant during this victorious phase. Functionaries complained about its declining influence and having 'little to do'.[5] As Defence Commissars, *Gauleiter* gained at least nominal authority over civil administration in all matters of homeland defence, which in these years mostly meant preparing for air raids. Theoretically, they also had substantial powers related to the war economy: deploying labour, allocating housing, enforcing rationing and even granting exemptions from military service. In practice, since they had to cooperate closely with military commanders, conflict and some chaos ensued. There was greater power to be gained in the occupied East. In Poland, even lower-ranking Party functionaries successfully dominated civil administration, achieving enormous authority despite lacking experience and qualifications.

If there was a common denominator to the experience of devout Nazis in this period, from Hitler down to the lowly Block Warden, it was that territorial expansion and war reinvigorated their ideological convictions and sense of purpose. Aggressive war in particular galvanized a movement that from the start had been devoted to struggle, both political and racial. With a new order on the horizon, its activists assumed radical positions against the representatives of the old social and political one.

Accomplices

The year 1938 was decisive in the relationship between the Nazis and the traditional, conservative elites. Thereafter, the latter's influence was severely curtailed, particularly in the spheres of military and foreign policy. Yet they continued to serve essential roles in German expansion, blurring the lines, never hard and fast, between the Nazis and these accomplices. With that year's shake-up of military leadership, Hitler replaced the conservative foreign minister he had retained from the last Weimar government, von Neurath, with Joachim von Ribbentrop. While still hoping Hitler's goals might be accomplished without war, his top diplomats were resigned to his plans or felt powerless to stop him. Within the military, men who supported bolder, aggressive policies now occupied key positions. Once Germany was at war, the generals accepted their exclusion from broad military strategy – setting goals in light of options and challenges – and focused on operational planning. The transformation of this former political elite into a merely functional one was complete.

Germany's top officers and generals stood ready to carry out the will of their highest superior, whose vision they largely shared. They supported Hitler's promise to annihilate the Polish state in principle, even though in practice some individual officers baulked at the brutality of SS and police actions. Most saw the Non-Aggression Pact with the Soviet Union as a major success. They credited Hitler with buying time, rescuing Germany from the prospect of a two-front war and gaining raw materials in the process. They also knew, because he so often repeated his intention, that the *Führer's* desire to crush the Soviet Union had not abated, reassuring the staunchest anti-communists among them.

There were some points of divergence between the Nazis and German military leaders in these years. They had genuine concerns about Germany's war readiness in late summer 1939. Only part of the Army was mechanized, tanks and aircraft were fewer and often inferior to British and French ones, and German reserves of critical supplies, like ammunition and oil, would likely last only months. Despite the success of the Polish campaign, there was doubt about invading France too soon and some urged a delay when Hitler broached plans for an attack that very autumn. After the fall of France the following summer, many became convinced that Hitler really did know best. Food and minerals from the Soviet Union, alongside fuel and other raw materials from Western countries, camouflaged economic problems. Arms production increased spectacularly, doubling between January and July 1940 alone.[6] The numbers of planes, submarines and tanks grew.

Ever-intensifying military production lined the pockets of Germany's big business elites. Motivated by the threat of state expropriation for not meeting targets, they strove to perform as the Nazis expected. Victory in France increased admiration for Hitler enormously in corporate circles. In the years to come, virtually all German companies contributed to the war effort in some way. Many began to benefit from the regime's various forced labour schemes involving Jews, prisoners of war and foreign workers. Although industry's large-scale exploitation of such labour had not yet started, some companies already revealed themselves as especially willing collaborators. The construction firm Hochtief, for example, embarked on a joint venture in 1940 with the *Gestapo* to open the first of the Work Education Camps for 'work shy' German and foreign workers. Its 650 internees suffered conditions so atrocious that a quarter could not regularly work, inspiring complaints from Hochtief managers about their performance.[7] Until 1941, the majority of forced labourers worked in agriculture. Landowners, especially the great estates, thus gained most advantage from the ever-increasing supply of workers.

The old conservative elites were no hindrance at all to the Nazis' radicalized measures against outsiders in this period. Among the judges, the 'euthanasia' programme sparked disquiet, but usually not for humanitarian reasons. Its lack of a proper legal foundation disturbed them, especially Justice Minister Gürtner. He responded by drafting actual laws for eliminating 'lives unworthy of life', which Hitler refused to sign. Gürtner nonetheless stayed on until his death in January 1941. Months before, he had suspended the lone German judge who protested 'euthanasia' openly within a judiciary that continued its enthusiastic service to the Nazi state.

Kristallnacht violence and damage elicited some dismay in elite circles but no active protests against antisemitic policy. There was extensive consensus here about dispossessing Jewish Germans,

Figure 3.2 The supervisory board of Degussa AG, a metals and chemical company, in 1936 (Courtesy of Evonik Industries AG, Corporate Archives, Hanau, Obj. no. 95.978).

especially once the regime clearly signalled its intention to do so. The proliferation of anti-Jewish legislation from 1938 to 1940 erased judicial anxiety as this became legalized theft. In the business world, a combination of private greed, commercial ambition and corporate competition drove the final push to 'Aryanize' before the state itself expropriated firms and properties. German companies ousted remaining Jewish board members and senior managers. Up and coming firms participated more enthusiastically than did longer-established ones, but all explored acquisition possibilities.

The start of the war marked a new stage in the complicity of certain intellectual elites. Doctors became killers, while studies by medical experts, including prominent psychiatrists, justified the murders. Chemists and other scientists experimented with more efficient methods of murder. The perpetrators of child and adult 'euthanasia' showed little remorse and even enjoyed certain benefits from taking German lives. Participating doctors gained choice professorial appointments at universities, frequently received government research grants and earned higher salaries for working at the 'euthanasia' centres. While not all physicians agreed with death as the only 'solution' to disability – some advocated curative education instead – they accepted the increasingly radicalized strategies of the Nazi state and adjusted their own attitudes to fit. Other academics gained new value for the regime in these years too. Historians, anthropologists, geographers and others involved in 'eastern research' legitimized not only the military conquest of Poland but also the brutal treatment of 'inferior' Slavs and Jews. Whether merging their own research agendas with the Nazis' racist one, perpetrating its crimes, furthering its geographical reach or profiting from these, Germany's elites were deeply complicit in the wrongs committed under the swastika.

Supporters

In 1938, Austrians and Sudetenlanders joined other Germans inside the Third Reich. Photographs in March and October captured their ecstatic responses to the soldiers' arrival; Hitler's visits sparked even greater euphoria. The majority supported annexation but affinity for Nazism alone does not explain their joyful reaction. In Austria, many socialists, liberals and conservatives alike shared long-held desires for the political unification of German speakers. In a country whose population was 90 per cent Catholic, the Catholic bishops' endorsement was especially influential. Desire for the dramatic economic improvements seen in Germany and an end to the fraught politics of recent years was significant as well. In Austria, a new crop of 'March violets' – opportunistic new Nazi Party members – bloomed. In the Sudetenland, per capita NSDAP and SA membership was significantly higher than in the Old Reich. These latest supporters solidified their new collective identity as Greater Germans through their treatment of outsiders; antisemitic shaming rituals, intimidation and violence surged. Within months, unemployment virtually disappeared in Austria thanks to economic investment from Berlin. That Reich Germans (German citizens before 1938) occupied certain plum political positions caused resentment, but Austrians quickly occupied top roles in the SS, as Reich Governors and *Gauleiter*, and gratitude to the *Führer* remained high overall.

Figure 3.3 A warm welcome for Hitler in Vienna (Austria) on 15 March 1938 (Everett Collection Historical/Alamy Stock Photo).

Reich Germans revealed their position on the Austrian annexation in the results of a single-question referendum held the next month. Hitler had used this technique before to secure evidence of popular approval retroactively, for example, after the Rhineland remilitarization in March 1936. Now ballots asked if there was agreement with Hitler's 'reunification' of Austria with the German Reich. Ninety-nine per cent of voters ticked 'yes', an obvious choice since the accompanying circle was at least three times larger than the negative alternative.

Once war began, shared external enemies cemented connections between old and new supporters, although there was initial common anxiety. The British-French declaration of war was deeply distressing to most; they had become used to spectacular foreign policy successes without bloodshed. Only twenty years had passed since the Great War and memories of suffering were still fresh. Fear and resignation quickly turned to relief as *Blitzkrieg* destroyed Poland, something to which few Germans objected, including those who did not support the Nazis.

Historians offer different assessments of the war's early impact on daily lives and material conditions. Some stress an immediate drop in living standards with the introduction of rationing; others, noting that limitations on foods and consumer goods in Nazi Germany were not new, emphasize continuities as victories mounted. Both are correct, with variation largely dependent on region and timing. Crucially, too, since Germany had essentially been on a war footing since 1936, continuities were with pre-1939 *warlike* economic conditions, not genuinely *peacetime* ones.[8]

From 1 September 1939, Germans were on high alert. Schoolchildren practiced with gas masks. Streetlights went off at night and windows were blacked out. Within weeks, with no active hostilities along Germany's border with France, everyday life resumed. Of course, tensions were higher along that western border, but the fall of France eased those almost totally. Overnight stays during the 1940 summer tourist season were up 35 per cent from the previous year, as Germans enjoyed vacationing in the vastly expanded Reich.[9] That summer marked the very highpoint of Hitler's popularity among 'ordinary' insiders. Praise for his seemingly superhuman achievements was heard in all circles.

Crucially, despite reductions in consumption, Germans were not going hungry as they had in the last war. Conquered territories provided foodstuffs as they bolstered morale. Many benefitted directly from the foods and goods soldiers shipped home, which strengthened support for Hitler's war aims. That casualties had yet to impact German families significantly also played a role. Life at home felt 'exactly the same', noted a soldier on leave. 'Only the absence of fathers and brothers' – and obituaries in the newspaper – 'reminded us that we were at war', one young boy observed.[10]

The war elided certain differences between Germans and created new bonds between them. Catholics felt less ostracized after Hitler's order to end provocations against the churches in September 1939. Their long-expressed patriotism rewarded, agitation against the regime diminished. Cheering victories and tracking *Wehrmacht* advances also unified Germans young and old. Veterans contrasted their experiences of interminable trench warfare with the speed of *Blitzkrieg* assaults.

German children enthusiastically pushed swastika pins into maps of Europe and applauded newsreel footage from the front. Hostilities brought Germans together by investing causes for grumbling, such as shortages or shoddy *ersatz* goods, with new meaning. They shared experiences of death and grief as well. Finally, attitudes to external enemies, as to outsiders within, provided common ground. By the end of 1940, majority Germans under Hitler had never been so united.

Commitment to the national war effort could coexist with uneven attitudes towards Nazi management of the circumstances of daily life. German workers' discontent certainly did not disappear. In fact, many persons labouring in war-related industries saw living standards plunge with the War Economy Decree in September 1939 aimed at a massive increase in armaments production. This meant longer hours, an intensified work pace, the abolition of higher pay for overtime and weekend work, the suspension of vacation rights and wage freezes. Yet even sharp dissatisfaction did not erupt into outright rebellion, in part because workers retained some degree of individual bargaining power. In 1939, 22 per cent of the German workforce served the military's needs; by 1940, 50 per cent did.[11] Their labour was desperately needed, especially before foreign workers began to fill shortages.

As German blood was shed to conquer foreign soil, Nazi promises of a new peasant nobility seemed emptier than ever. Call-ups to the front severely exacerbated the agricultural labour crisis, which was so bad in 1940 that children were taken out of school to help with the harvest. Foreign workers and prisoners of war only partially alleviated the situation. Much to the chagrin of Nazi authorities, farming families in both smaller villages and on great estates sometimes treated these foreigners, even 'inferior' Poles, as equals, inviting them to eat at their table and attend church together. While there is evidence that agricultural communities resented the regime for demonizing these practices, farmers were spared many of the effects of rationing and enjoyed the relative safety of the countryside. Wartime service offered young farm workers an escape from narrow provincial lives and chances for advancement in the military. German victory also held the promise of farms of their own on newly conquered land.

Women already made up one-third of Germany's workforce in 1939. With the invasion of Poland, working-class women were moved in large numbers from non-essential to essential labour. With men at the front, there were increased higher-paid opportunities for them. By contrast, the Nazi regime was reluctant to conscript middle-class women into the war economy, fearing negative consequences for morale. Mobilizing them proceeded much more slowly. War affected German women's lives in four other respects as well. First, they spent more time queuing to shop. Seeing this as serving a greater patriotic purpose minimized complaints, as did fear of expressing disloyalty at war, something the Nazis promised to punish harshly. Second, they missed absent sons, husbands, brothers and fathers, and mourned the fallen ones. Third, as 'Aryan' women they became vulnerable to accusations of fraternization with male foreign workers and prisoners of war, far more than when the genders were reversed.

Finally, some women became more deeply involved in making Nazi terror work. This includes those who became perpetrators of oppression and violence, notably during *Kristallnacht*. They were not silent bystanders to the carnage but cheered and jeered along with men and children. 'Aryan' women stole paintings, money, furs, silverware, and even wine and food from stores and private homes. They humiliated elderly Jews in front of crowds and pointed out targets to roving bands of SA men. Some women also enforced conformity with Nazi ideals via denunciations and as witnesses in preliminary investigations and court trials, whatever their individual motives. A very small number of women served as 'SS Helpers' guarding the Lichtenburg camp for women from 1937 to its closure in 1939, when positions opened at Ravensbrück, a new concentration camp exclusively for female prisoners. Job advertisements lured candidates with descriptions of the 'light physical work' involved in overseeing women who had 'committed offences against the Volksgemeinschaft'.[12] Most applicants were aged twenty-one to forty-five, poorly educated and often from the rural lower class. As camp guards, they earned less than an average unskilled factory worker, but much more than a domestic servant or even a trained cook. To keep the job, women had to accept, and be willing to carry out, beating and humiliating the inmates. Although overall they never made up more than 10 per cent of Nazi concentration camp personnel, their complicity in this area is noteworthy.

The most dramatic shift in female perpetrator roles took place once the war began. Nurses had known about and assisted in sterilizations. Now they collaborated in 'euthanasia'. Male physicians turned on the gas at the killing centres, but female nurses accompanied adult victims on transports and walked them to the doors. They left children to starve and die from neglect, administered sedative drugs resulting in pneumonia and, in a later phase of Nazi 'euthanasia', injected psychiatric patients with fatal doses of chemicals. A monthly bonus ensured their silence. A few women requested transfers to other facilities. Some later justified their actions, saying they had merely released victims from suffering, while others maintained they needed the income. Many, as one post-war defendant claimed, gave it 'hardly any thoughts', so thoroughly had they adopted the Nazi world view that these were 'lives unworthy of life'.[13]

For young German males, donning an armed forces uniform became a mass experience from September 1939: 85 per cent of German men aged twenty to thirty and declared fit served in some capacity. For many, the prospect of combat after years of 'practicing' was exciting.[14] Soldiers' attitudes differed sharply from the generally apprehensive German population. The experience ultimately proved exhilarating for some, but losing friends to enemy-inflicted injuries or being wounded themselves tempered their excitement. Despite the successes of *Blitzkrieg*, over 100,000 members of the German military had been killed by the end of 1940.[15]

The notion of a 'clean' *Wehrmacht* fighting a 'normal' war, different from the racial war of the SS, endured for decades after 1945. It was a myth. Soldiers expressed little remorse at Polish civilian deaths and witnessed mass shootings first-hand; they were also under orders to cooperate with the SS and police units arriving to crush the possibility of organized resistance, particularly by the Polish ruling elite. Soldiers massacred supposed 'partisans' in concert with these forces and perpetrated atrocities on their own against unarmed Polish prisoners of war and civilians, including Jews and Roma.

For many German soldiers, their first contact with Eastern Jews and *shtetls* (small Jewish villages) corroborated Nazi propaganda about difference and dirt; their letters home noted that Jews here looked just as they did in The Stormer (*Der Stürmer*), a violently antisemitic Nazi newspaper. In these often impoverished places, there was less to steal, although in larger towns, soldiers grabbed jewellery, furs and even furniture to send home. Soldiers' experiences in France were different. Though the advances through the Ardennes had been long and exhausting and they mourned comrades who had been killed, the spoils of victory were immense. The German military occupation forces lived 'like gods in France', as the common saying went. There was no rationing, and due to a highly unequal exchange rate, soldiers could get anything, in whatever quantities, they wanted. They sent provisions and gifts back to Germany, and brought more home with them on leave. They even became tourists, taking in the sights. The Army enjoyed these fruits of war disproportionately. *Luftwaffe* pilots failed to dominate the British Royal Air Force and suffered heavy casualties. German sailors also saw substantial losses in Norway and the Navy's surface vessels were no match for the British. By 1940, though, the number of U-Boats ready to inflict damage on key Atlantic shipping routes had more than doubled. The young submarine captains feted in Nazi propaganda foresaw future victories.

With the country at war, there was consensus among Hitler's supporters about their external enemies. Little sympathy existed for Poles as 'inferior' Slavs and for Poland as an allegedly artificial creation of the detested Versailles Treaty. Nazi propaganda claiming the mistreatment of German minorities was widely believed. Thus, the invasion of Poland was considered necessary to save fellow Germans. Enduring admiration for French culture in no way minimized exultation at defeating Germany's historic enemy. Even the most devout Anglophiles within the educated classes, with their respect for English literature and British imperial power, blamed the British for continuing the war by refusing Hitler's offer of peace. Some Germans followed the latest Nazi propaganda line, which attributed British stubbornness to Jews pulling the strings in London.

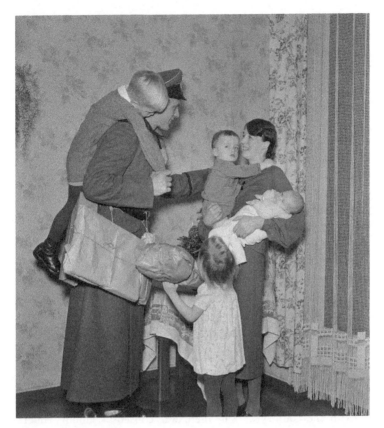

Figure 3.4 A German soldier bearing gifts arrives home for Christmas in 1940 (bpk Bildagentur/Liselotte Orgel-Köhne (Purper)/Art Resource, New York).

Supporters' attitudes to outsiders at home were more varied throughout 1938 to 1940. Questions persist about their responses to *Kristallnacht*. To what degree were 'ordinary' Germans involved as perpetrators? What role did witnesses play? What did most Germans think about the treatment of Jewish Germans, not only on that night of broken glass but also in the months that followed? Not surprisingly, the answers to all three questions are complicated. In some places, Nazis led the actions; elsewhere, other Germans played a more active, or even the dominant, role. For example, in many communities in rural Württemberg, SA men carried out the attacks alone. By contrast, in Breslau (now Wrocław, Poland), an eyewitness observed, 'These were all civilians. The police, the SS, and the Storm Troopers were nowhere to be seen.'[16] Other research contradicts that picture, reversing the generalizations about rural areas and urban centres. Whether we explain spectators' passivity as stemming from fear, disinterest or helplessness, their motivations meant nothing to the victims. Inaction worsened their situation by permitting the violence to continue. Moreover, spectating could also be a more engaged experience; onlookers applauded, laughed and chanted, even if they did not hurl a stone, deface a storefront or steal anything.

Nonetheless, the majority German population seems to have reacted negatively to the November pogrom. 'Are we upright Germans or just a mob?', one woman asked disgustedly in her diary.[17] Some were so dismayed they denounced assailants, vandals and thieves to the police. Others assisted Jews by providing food, shelter and loans of household objects to replace those destroyed or stolen. They warned Jewish neighbours about impending arrests, and even, infrequently, hid them from the *Gestapo*. At the same time, there were almost no cases of open opposition to *Kristallnacht*. Any fear the events provoked turned inwards: non-Jewish Germans worried about what might happen not to the Jews but to themselves. Catholics warned each other that it might be their turn. Property damage inspired more outrage than physical violence, mass arrests or concentration camp internment. The public generally did not condemn the final mass wave of expropriation that followed the November pogrom. Some Germans who had not already taken advantage now hurried to line their own pockets. In sum, then, Hitler's supporters backed the exclusion and expulsion of Jews from the economy, but not excessive open violence against them, especially if it involved property destruction. The Nazi regime took note of that response. It would devise less public but more radical solutions to the 'Jewish Question' accordingly.

By 1939, the peak year of Jewish emigration, few Germans still had contacts with Jews. They no longer had to think much about them, so complete was their social segregation. By contrast, the 'euthanasia' of disabled Germans, an increasingly open secret, touched many families directly. It took place on German soil, within German towns, close enough to see and smell the smoke from the crematoria and even hear screams. Rumours about suspicious death notices and deliveries of urns of ashes made the rounds, especially in smaller communities: death from appendicitis, for example, in a patient whose appendix had been removed years earlier. Some institution administrators witnessed the extermination process first-hand. Children playing near Hadamar, a psychiatric hospital and killing centre, chanted songs about the 'murder buses' that transported victims. Nazi officials acknowledged that talk of mass murder was spreading like wildfire. However, popular unease and disquiet was not active opposition and it had no effect at this stage. Moreover, a silent majority presumably agreed that, in many cases, these lives were indeed 'unworthy'. Their concerns, as during *Kristallnacht*, were selfish ones. Recalling Great War shortages, some supporters wondered whether the killings of 'useless eaters' meant food supplies were dwindling. The elderly and severely injured war veterans worried they might be next.

Racial and social outsiders

Expansion and war exacerbated the oppression of outsiders within the Greater German Reich. The situation worsened most dramatically for two groups: Jews and the disabled. For most Jewish Germans, the events of 1938 – particularly the open violence of the pogrom and total economic strangulation that followed – made it *the* fateful year in their lives under Hitler. In many ways, however, the pogrom might be considered less a dramatic break with previous Nazi strategies to solve the 'Jewish Question' than the 'culmination' of an already 'brutal trajectory'.[18] Physical threats and assaults had never stopped, even in the relatively quiet years, and the 'de-Jewification' and 'Aryanization' of the economy had intensified almost a year before. In the months leading up to 9 November, Jews already faced radically amplified antisemitic legislation, property damage, public humiliations and open violence.

Much of this took place in Austria and the Sudetenland, but in June 1938, Berliners also witnessed a wave of antisemitic riots and vandalism instigated by Nazi Party members and inspired by Goebbels-led propaganda. That same month, an estimated 1,500 male Jews were arrested for being 'work shy' and sent to concentration camps. Most had a criminal record, though usually only for minor violations of the myriad laws to which they were increasingly subject. Few Jews in Germany remained hopeful that their situation might improve, but the pogrom was nevertheless a major shock. It marked a watershed in all their lives, whatever the differences in their previous experiences.

The shattered windows of over 10,000 stores gave rise to the name *Kristallnacht*. Countless memoirs, Nazi reports and witness testimonies describe the broken glass. Two thousand synagogues burned that night as well. These public actions have obscured another, less well-known facet of that horrific night: the widespread destruction of private homes. There is no reliable figure for how many houses and apartments were invaded, vandalized and damaged, although it was many times higher than stores and synagogues. In Vienna, for example, possibly 70 per cent of Jewish domiciles were raided. Whether the perpetrators were SA men, Hitler Youth or even neighbours, the effects were usually the same: 'No cup was left unbroken, no window left intact,' one victim recalled. Another remembered sledge hammers used 'to destroy everything'; they 'spilled ink on paintings, rugs and tablecloths, and cut blankets with glass shards'.[19] Many dwellings became uninhabitable. The wanton destruction of their last safe refuge inflicted a devastating material and psychological toll on Jews in Greater Germany. Even worse, terrifying bodily violence, sometimes fatal, accompanied these home invasions. Men suffered this more often, but women and girls were not spared physical attacks, sexual assaults and murder. The perpetrators also harmed 'Aryan' women married to Jewish men.

The 30,000 Jewish men arrested during the pogrom and sent to Dachau, Buchenwald and Sachsenhausen faced horrific abuses and deprivations. The severe effects of their experiences manifested themselves on their faces and bodies. Their descriptions of their

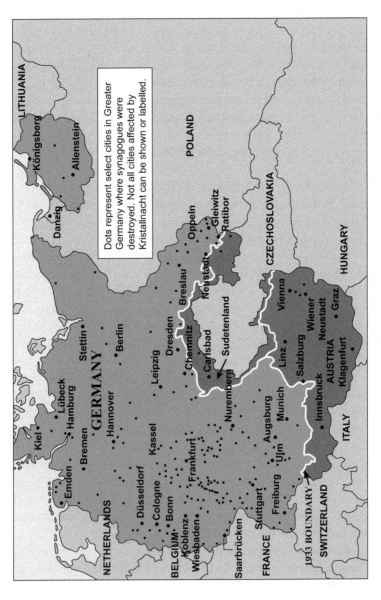

Map 3. Synagogues destroyed during the *Kristallnacht* pogrom, 9–10 November 1938. (This redrawn map is based on one the United States Holocaust Memorial Museum gave permission to reproduce.)

Figure 3.5 A Jewish shopkeeper cleans up broken glass after *Kristallnacht*, 9–10 November 1938 (Hulton Archive/Stringer via Getty Images).

Figure 3.6 A private home in Vienna destroyed on *Kristallnacht* (bpk Bildagentur/Art Resource, New York).

homecomings echoed one another: 'I didn't look like the same man.'[20] Although internment was temporary this time, their circumstances after release were dire. Already by the start of 1938, professionals like doctors and lawyers were largely shut out of the German economy; their clientele could only include Jews. Half of all Jewish workers were unemployed. Those who still had jobs worked for Jewish employers. As their businesses folded or were 'Aryanized', employment prospects dwindled further. The flood of ordinances, decrees and laws that followed *Kristallnacht* – there were 229 before the outbreak of war – made the situation immeasurably worse. By early 1939, approximately 75–80 per cent of Jewish businesses open in 1933 were in 'Aryan' hands.[21]

Even as utter destitution loomed, the increased social isolation could be even more painful. Certain streets were out of bounds; theatres, concerts, cinemas and museums off limits; and public school attendance denied. The desire to leave Germany was now near universal, the destination unimportant. Despite the regime's efforts to accelerate emigration (while simultaneously expropriating all Jewish assets), finding a country willing to accept them was often impossible. Under these circumstances, in the ten months after the pogrom, 115,000 Jewish Germans managed to leave, 10,000 of them children under sixteen whose parents made the agonizing decision to send them to Great Britain via the Children's Transport rescue mission.[22] Those who remained were disproportionately older and female.

The war worsened their conditions immediately. Discriminatory rationing policies – their cards were embossed with a large 'J' – restricted what foodstuffs and clothing Jewish Germans could buy and when they could shop. Since spring 1939, Jews could be evicted without notice. Their already critical housing shortage deteriorated further when the regime forced some into overcrowded 'Jew houses', apartments designated for Jewish tenants only. All Jewish men aged eighteen to fifty-five and Jewish women aged eighteen to fifty had to register for forced labour. The number one consequence of the outbreak of war, however, was minimizing avenues for escape. Hostilities closed many routes over land and sea, while new visa requirements multiplied. Deliveries of letters and parcels often ceased, which left Jewish Germans feeling increasingly cut off from the outside world. The Nazis even confiscated their radios after the invasion of Poland. Still, most hardly imagined their very lives were in danger.

The lives of disabled Germans clearly were. The 'euthanasia' murders were not 'good deaths' as the term literally means. Babies and toddlers up to the age of three, the initial victims of child 'euthanasia', were too young to leave many individual traces in the historical record beyond a few photographs. Without their voices, we rely on their parents, medical professionals and authorities to reconstruct their experiences. After local physicians or midwives officially registered disabled children's names, and three physicians decided whether they should live or die, parents received 'requests' to send them to a designated facility or special paediatric ward for 'treatment'. These were regularly distant from family homes to discourage visiting. Some parents agreed to these requests, for a variety of reasons. Mothers sought respite from the demands of caring for a disabled child alongside their other children while managing work or a farm, especially with husbands away at the front. Families felt endangered by the stigma attached to a 'hereditarily ill' child; removing them might be safer for all. Others likely believed – and trusted – that specialized treatment might actually improve their children's conditions. The state's promise to pay the associated costs was an added incentive. Some parents, suspecting or even knowing their children's ultimate fate, genuinely wanted an end to their suffering if they believed them to be in pain. However, for the vast majority, accepting institutionalization was not consent to murder. They sought healing, not death.

For all Germans in psychiatric care, young and old, the war brought increased hunger. By January 1940, at most state institutions, daily provisions were half those of the pre-war years and those had usually been minimal. Adults deemed 'incurable' faced further dietary restrictions before their transfer to the 'euthanasia' centres. On appointed dates, trucks, vans or the infamous grey buses arrived to transport patients. The sight of these triggered enormous anxiety. Patients wrote home, 'I live in fear again, because the cars were here again.'[23] Those temporarily spared mourned the loss of their friends.

The scenes described by medical staff on transport days suggest victims had some foreknowledge of their fate. Patients shouted and cried, and clung to the nursing sisters as they were loaded onto the vehicles. Upon arrival, victims had to strip naked for a brief physical examination to determine the fictitious cause of death. Office staff confirmed their identity; others took photographs. Nurses led them to a gas chamber disguised as a shower room, which held up to sixty patients at one time. A physician turned on the gas tap to release carbon monoxide into the room, watching at a small window in the wall until these Germans had suffocated to death. Victims screamed, and pounded on the door and walls. There was nothing humane about the process, which could take twenty minutes or even longer.

'Euthanasia' also threatened 'asocial' Germans, and a series of measures in 1938 aimed at 'crime prevention' further intensified their vulnerability. Labour shortages as the country geared up for war meant the 'work shy' received special attention. In June, the *Gestapo* arrested some 10,000 men – Jews and Sinti and Roma among them – in

Figure 3.7 Smoke rises from the crematorium at the Hadamar 'euthanasia' centre, *c*.1941 (Courtesy of Diözesanarchiv Limburg (DAL) 7.2.1., Nachlass Pfr. Hans Becker/Wilhelm Reusch).

mass raids and sent them to concentration camps. This round-up, 'Operation Work Shy', targeted men who had long been on police and welfare authorities' radar. Most came from lower-class, impoverished backgrounds. Often ostracized by their families, suffering alcohol or drug addiction, and, in many cases, years of prolonged joblessness during the Depression, they had difficulty integrating into the workforce. Now they were punished.

The raids continued that summer and throughout the first years of the war. Victims included German women who had allegedly failed to adapt to community norms. From early 1939 to early 1940, one in four women sent to the newly established Ravensbrück concentration camp wore the black triangles marking out 'asocial' prisoners. Those who survived rarely spoke about their experiences; most were too ashamed to acknowledge the 'crime' that led them there. However, some left traces in the records. For example, Else Krug, a prostitute, became a *Kapo* at Ravensbrück – an inmate appointed to oversee others in various tasks – though one who defiantly refused to beat fellow prisoners. Else's mother had no idea of her location before she was murdered in a 'euthanasia' centre in 1942. Other 'asocial' prisoners wrote heartbreaking letters home, begging for 'just one word' from their families: 'I'm so unhappy', one concluded.[24] 'Asocial' victims included lesbians, showing that homosexuality remained extremely dangerous in Nazi Germany. Although the regime's persecution of gay men had passed its peak years by 1939, their arrests continued and once imprisoned, gay men now rarely gained their freedom.

From 1938 onwards, and even more once the war began, Nazi Germany became home to large numbers of foreigners. As non-Germans, their experiences of, and responses to, the Nazi regime lie beyond the scope of this book. Yet since Germans' lives were increasingly marked by their interactions with this large and growing group, some brief comments are in order. First came foreign workers, then prisoners of war. The former volunteered, at least initially; later, like the prisoners, the majority were forced to labour for the Third Reich, most of them as agricultural workers. To begin with, because so economically necessary, these foreigners were not treated terribly; however, with 1.2 million prisoners of war from France alone at the Nazis' disposal, a seemingly limitless supply allowed ideological considerations to determine their treatment.[25] Foreign workers from Western Europe generally experienced better conditions, though, not surprisingly, they had no right to vacations or pay raises, and received paltry wages. Restrictions on the approximately one million Polish labourers in Germany – whether voluntary or forced – were more severe. They had to wear a letter 'P' badge at all times, were subject to curfews and were barred from public transport, cinemas, most restaurants, and attending church services with Germans. Nazi propaganda depicted them as a threat, but isolated on different farms, under surveillance and demoralized by worry about families at home, concerted resistance was extremely unlikely.

Resisters

As Germany became 'Greater', the number of those opposed to it grew. Resistance to Hitler flared immediately in the territories it absorbed, as well as in countries it directly occupied. In the Old Reich itself, the contours of organized resistance underwent a transformation between 1938 and 1940. Organized leftist opposition practically ceased. The Social Democratic leadership-in-exile, now in Paris, called a formal halt to activities in 1939. Even distributing leaflets and newspapers, it said, was futile and too dangerous. SOPADE's *Reports from Germany* on popular opinion ended the following year. The Soviet Union's signing of the Non-Aggression Pact, viewed by some as cooperation with fascism, left German communists confused, disillusioned and paralysed. Their activities across the Greater German Reich were soon insignificant.

By contrast, sporadic dissent within some conservative circles, even those once supportive of Hitler, now morphed into outright plotting. Lieutenant Colonel Hans Oster, long critical of the *Führer* state, was at the centre of the best known of these. Oster worked for Germany's Military Intelligence Organization. By early 1938, as war with Czechoslovakia and the threat of a major European conflict loomed, his determination to remove Hitler and restructure the political system solidified. The men around him agreed: once accomplices, they now became resisters to avoid war. Among them were both military figures and civilians, including Colonel General Ludwig Beck, who resigned as Army Chief of General Staff in summer 1938, and former Leipzig mayor Carl Goerdeler. They planned a *putsch* by a small group of officers, although not all agreed Hitler should be killed. By preventing immediate war, the Munich Agreement of 30 September 1938 undermined their scheme. Hitler's subsequent dizzying victories largely stemmed conservative opposition. Yet, for a very few, the resolve to act in the future never wavered.

Munich Agreement

By the end of 1937, Hitler was set on the destruction of Czechoslovakia. A growing movement in the Czech Sudetenland – an industrial area bordering Germany that had a German majority – clamoured to 'come home to the Reich'. Fearing war, Britain and France sought to appease Hitler. Their leaders, Neville Chamberlain and Édouard Daladier, met with Hitler and Italy's Benito Mussolini in Munich on 29–30 September 1938 to decide Czechoslovakia's fate. The Munich Agreement handed the Sudetenland to Nazi Germany. Munich represented a victory of sorts for Hitler: he had gained important resources and Czechoslovakia was left practically defenceless; in another sense, however, it was a setback, since it denied him the opportunity to smash Czechoslovakia by force.

As before, Germany's Churches responded to events in the Third Reich with dissent in some areas, accommodation in others and fundamental loyalty overall. Despite some parallels in Catholic and Protestant opposition, there was no unified, coordinated action between them. Few pastors openly condemned *Kristallnacht* violence from the pulpit, although many privately deplored the destruction of synagogues. Neither Church formally condemned the 'euthanasia' programme in this period. Individual Christians tried to thwart Nazi racial persecution, at least in specific cases, by forging identity documents or intentionally falsifying patient information. Some clergy members, unable to square Nazi crimes with Christian teaching, now reluctantly turned to opposing the state itself, not only its interference in religious affairs. They believed, as Confessing Church pastor Dietrich Bonhoeffer had already stated in 1933, that merely 'bandaging' the victims fallen under the Nazi 'wheel' was not enough; instead, a spoke must be put 'into the wheel itself'.[26] Bonhoeffer joined the Military Intelligence Organization, where he, alongside other like-minded men, compiled files on Nazi atrocities. His active fight against Hitler had begun.

The number of insiders actively resisting the Nazis overall remained exceedingly small, but the Nazis treated even youthful nonconformity extremely harshly, and more so once the nation was at war. For instance, young Germans who wore English fashions and danced to jazz music at underground clubs – the Swing Youth – were among those arrested and sent to new 'youth protection camps', such as one at Moringen, which, from autumn 1940, interned boys as young as sixteen.

Racial and social outsiders had no choice but to defend themselves as their freedom, livelihoods and very lives faced greater threats. They continued to engage in all kinds of activities that challenged Nazi actions, values and aims, including deliberately breaking the laws against them. Some Jewish Germans refused to use the middle names 'Sara' or 'Israel' on official paperwork (as mandated since 1938) or hand over their radios. They broke curfews, visited forbidden places and ignored limited shopping hours. They transferred assets abroad despite prohibitions. They sat defiantly on park benches marked 'Only for Aryans'.[27] Defending themselves physically was rare, but not unheard of. During *Kristallnacht*, for example, some Jews fought back against their tormentors. Others, feeling their lives were not worth saving, took their own. There was a wave of Jewish suicides across the Reich after November 1938 as there had been in Germany in 1933 when the Nazis came to power and again in Vienna after annexation.

Figure 3.8 Lizi Rosenfeld, a Jewish woman, sits defiantly on a bench marked 'Only for Aryans' in Vienna, August 1938 (United States Holocaust Memorial Museum, courtesy of Leo Spitzer).

These years saw a dramatic shift in the communal response of the newly renamed Reich Association of Jews in Germany, now overseen directly by the Ministry of the Interior. The earlier educational and cultural work was now largely viewed as pointless and energy-wasting. Instead, focus turned almost exclusively to facilitating emigration, petitioning authorities to amend dispossession policies and caring for those left behind. The Jewish Culture League also outlasted the outbreak of war, but its activities were severely circumscribed.

In the wake of Operation Work Shy (June 1938), Sinti and Roma wives and mothers, like Jewish women after the November pogrom, wrote petitions and made personal visits to police stations and government offices, demanding their male relatives' release from camps. Some were even successful. The relatives of psychiatric patients similarly sent a flood of correspondence requesting information about their loved ones, asking for visitation rights or their return from institutions, and challenging official explanations for their deaths. Several individuals tried to press charges, unsuccessfully, against hospitals they accused of foul play or demanded better rations for the patients. Some, at least temporarily, refused to send their children to the special paediatric wards. Threatened with loss of custody rights or forcible removal from their homes, they relented. Patients also tried to save their own lives. They drew attention to what was happening during their transfers to the 'euthanasia' centres, announcing to onlookers they were about to be murdered. Knowing transfers were coming, victims ran away from psychiatric hospitals. Such resistance spared some lives, though very few. Still, these courageous rescue and survival efforts, like all the individual and collective acts described above, challenge any notion of meek submission to Nazi power.

CHAPTER 4
DESCENT (1941–1943)

In hindsight, 1941 can be seen as the year Nazi Germany lost the war. At the time, that seemed impossible: by late summer, Adolf Hitler controlled more of Europe and beyond than any ruler since Napoleon. Invasion of the Soviet Union (Operation Barbarossa), to which Hitler's attention turned immediately after the defeat of France in 1940, finally came on 22 June 1941, after German forces had already fought in North Africa, Yugoslavia and Greece. Barbarossa was to be no 'normal' war. The notorious 'Commissar Order', issued by the German High Command prior to the invasion, authorized summary executions of certain populations. As well, four SS Special Task Forces followed the *Wehrmacht*, murdering alleged Jewish, Roma and Slavic partisans, thus escalating the 'Holocaust by bullets' first initiated in Poland. Hundreds of thousands of men, women and children died at their hands. Millions of Soviet prisoners of war also perished in German captivity.

Germans continued to be murdered in both the child and adult 'euthanasia' programs, despite Hitler's formal halt to the latter in August 1941. At some point that autumn – the exact timing will never be known – and after the process had already begun at regional levels, the *Führer* signalled his preference for physical extermination as the 'Final Solution of the Jewish Question', first of Soviet Jews, and then all Jews in Europe. Extermination also became the Nazis' favoured method for solving the 'Gypsy Problem'. Descent into mechanized murder was the next step. By late 1941, 'special vans' were operating in Poland. These trucks asphyxiated victims, fifty to seventy at a time, by pumping carbon monoxide into their sealed cargo compartments. By January 1942, gas chambers using Zyklon B, a pesticide, were ready for use at Auschwitz-Birkenau, the largest of the Nazis' extermination

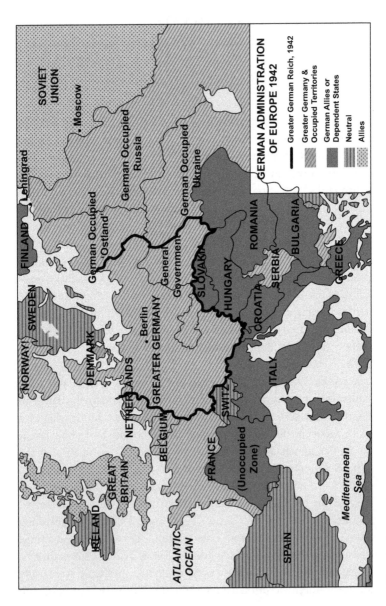

Map 4. Greater Germany in 1942.

camps. That same month, Reinhard Heydrich convened the Wannsee Conference in Berlin to coordinate measures for the 'Final Solution'. Jews across Europe were to be systematically slaughtered or worked to death. Five additional SS-run death camps started operations in the General Government (Poland) by the end of the year: Bełżec, Chełmno, Majdanek, Sobibór and Treblinka. By then the first Jews from the Reich and the Protectorate were being transported to be murdered in the East.

Nazi Germany's military fortunes turned with the stalling of the offensive outside Moscow in December 1941. At the same time, Hitler's decision to declare war on the United States on 11 December 1941, four days after the Japanese attack on Pearl Harbor, signalled the beginning of the end for his ambitions to make Germany a global power. Despite efforts in 1942 to conclude his eastern campaign successfully before America could intervene in the European war, the year closed with defeat looming in the Battle of Stalingrad. That defeat, formalized by the surrender of the German Sixth Army in February 1943, meant Hitler could not win the war in the East. Germany faced a far superior alliance of Soviet, American, British and Commonwealth forces impossible for it to overcome.

By May 1943, when Tunis fell to the Allies, Germany lost control of North Africa. What remained to Hitler, as the Allies invaded Italy and gained the upper hand in the Battle of the Atlantic and in massive bombing raids on German cities, was a stubborn and bloody eastern retreat. At home, the Nazi regime urged commitment to 'total war' as the only hope of final victory. Germans responded by doing what they could to survive what 'total war' entailed.

Nazis

With the invasion of the Soviet Union, the *Führer* state became one from which the *Führer* himself was increasingly absent. His visits to Berlin and Bavaria from his eastern commander headquarters became rare. He delivered far fewer public speeches and radio addresses. While he distanced himself from the *Volk*, his approach to directing the war became even more hands-on. He personally oversaw operational timing and tactics, above all in the East. Hitler's strategy in launching Operation Barbarossa took ideological, military and material factors into consideration. Communism had to be vanquished and the Slavic 'subhumans' subdued. With German control over the oil and grain fields on which the Reich now depended, autarky could finally become a reality. Looking ahead, he imagined that Germany would be ready for an inevitable battle with the Americans, having first defeated the Soviet Union. With his ally Japan now attacking British possessions in the Pacific, Hitler believed that Britain would finally seek peace terms, and he could avoid a two-front war.

In retrospect, Hitler's 'fatal miscalculations' as a wartime commander in this period are clear.[1] They arose in large part not because he was the hopeless military bungler some histories depict, but because political and ideological imperatives weighed more heavily for him than strictly military considerations. Hitler's choices – including those made on the Eastern Front and his declaration of war on the United States – emerged from hubris-driven underestimations of enemy military potential and a consuming desire always to dictate timing himself. Hitler's hands were all over these decisions; not surprisingly, he took no responsibility for the defeats that resulted. Those were the generals' fault. He also blamed his Axis partners, especially Italy. Eventually Hitler turned on the *Volk* itself.

With regard to the 'Final Solution', Hitler's precise fingerprints are more difficult to detect. He deliberately hid his own role here: there were no written decrees ordering the extermination of the European Jews and while his public threats were remarkably transparent, he did not always speak frankly even within his inner circle. Ultimately, the 'Final Solution' – systematic mass murder – was impossible without Hitler, but he authorized more than he personally initiated. He was aware of its scale and scope; all the details he left to others. Unlike his military generals, whom he distrusted, Hitler's Party henchmen had his confidence. He was certain they understood his goals and were ready to work toward them in the most radical way possible. For example, he approved Goebbels's request to make Jewish Germans wear the Star of David badge in September 1941, and, under pressure from Himmler, agreed to deport them, starting the following month, to ghettos, mass shooting sites and extermination camps in the East.

Even though this period saw the prospect of defeat become ever more likely, individual leading Nazis experienced personal and institutional successes. The invasion of the Soviet Union accelerated the timeline for SS dreams of a European 'new order', while massively expanding the SS power base, and with it, the power of Himmler. He was made Reich Minister of the Interior in August 1943. His key achievement in these years, one he described as a 'glorious page in our history' in a speech to SS leaders in Posen that autumn, was the transition from a mere territorial solution to the 'Jewish Question' to utter annihilation.[2] Unlike Hitler, Himmler witnessed Nazi crimes up close. A mass shooting in Minsk in August 1941 disturbed him; it was too taxing on the murderers, he concluded. The results of experiments at Auschwitz with Zyklon B, a pesticide, which he saw first-hand, assured him there was a better method. Although Himmler was not present at the Wannsee Conference on 20 January 1942, its outcomes were in tune with his intentions. Occupied Poland was to become the locus of the 'Final Solution'. There, European Jewry would be destroyed in purpose-built death camps as well as through mass shootings, which continued at every stage of the Holocaust.

Wannsee Conference

At this conference on 20 January 1942, held at a villa in the Berlin suburb of Wannsee, fifteen SS and government officials gathered over cognac and cigars to formalize and coordinate the 'Final Solution': the systematic, deliberate, physical extermination of Europe's Jews. The meeting was chaired by Reinhard Heydrich, head of the SS Security Service; Adolf Eichmann drafted the minutes. Neither Hitler nor Himmler attended. The meeting minutes do not mention killing specifically, but all men present were well aware of what phrases like 'transport to the East' and 'Final Solution' actually meant. The conference did not initiate mass murder; the mass shootings of Polish and Soviet Jews were already occurring and experiments with gassing techniques were underway. Instead, participants discussed how to implement a policy decided at the highest level of the Nazi regime. Administrative details confirmed at Wannsee included plans for exploiting Jewish labour ('a large number will doubtlessly be lost through natural reduction', Eichmann recorded) and setting targets: 11,000,000 European Jews from across the continent were to be worked to death or killed.

The SS economic empire had grown substantially since 1938, when its first enterprise, the German Earth and Stone Works, opened brickworks at Sachsenhausen to exploit inmate labour for direct SS profit. Camps built at stone and clay quarries followed. Now the SS Business and Administration Main Office oversaw integrating the concentration camps into the general war economy: by deploying inmates as slave labour and 'leasing' prisoners to outside firms involved in armaments production. Before it ended their lives, the SS organization extracted any possible value from Jewish victims, their labour as well as their assets. Individual SS men benefitted personally, whether as camp guards, Special Task Force shooters or death camp administrators. The belongings of victims – from jewellery to gold teeth removed from corpses – often found their way into SS hands, even though officially destined for the Reich. Opportunities for corruption and plunder helped offset any rare moral qualms. Shared acts of brutality also created a sense of belonging and new friendships that some recalled fondly after the war.[3]

Nazi Party functionaries instigated local, grassroots anti-Jewish initiatives, which in turn further radicalized national policy. Baldur von Schirach, now *Gauleiter* of Vienna, pushed the deportation of Reich Jews forward by advocating for a 'Jew-free' city. Goebbels, in his capacity as *Gauleiter* of Berlin, did the same. Hans Frank, head of the General Government, who had long objected to it being a dumping ground for unwanted Jews, pressed for annihilation. They were knocking on an open door, of course; Hitler sometimes delayed certain measures, but only for the short term.

The highest Nazi functionaries found their access to the *Führer* increasingly limited by Martin Bormann, Hitler's new personal secretary, who also ran the Nazi Party Chancellery (the NSDAP head office); however, they remained completely loyal to the man from whom all their power flowed. Hitler's words still inspired and united them, and memories of the pre-1933 'period of struggle' invigorated their efforts even as the war turned against Germany. Many Party functionaries who had felt useless while Germany was winning the war saw their roles in state and local government expand. The consequences of disloyalty were also no secret. Hitler threatened these explicitly when they gathered on the anniversaries of the 1923 *putsch* and 1933 seizure of power.

Hitler Youth members were similarly further enlisted and empowered. They now served the war effort more directly, for example, as *Luftwaffe* 'helpers', operating searchlights, sounding air raid warning signals and, eventually, operating anti-aircraft guns. The roster of activities left little time for classes even before bombs destroyed their schools. Whereas Hitler Youth service had once preceded a stint in the Reich Labour Service before conscription into the *Wehrmacht*, by August 1943, eighteen-year-old German boys were sent directly to the front. Schooled in fascist dogma for a decade, young Nazis felt proud to contribute. By contrast, the SA Brownshirts continued to resent how little recognition their efforts received and how minor their part in Germany's struggle was. Too old for the front, the 'old rowdies', as one SA man called them, had no desire to stay home 'to keep house': dispensing cigarettes to injured comrades in military hospitals, helping farmers with the harvest, fighting forest fires and resettling ethnic Germans fleeing the Red Army's advance.[4]

SA grievances were not unique among Nazis in this period, although fanaticism insulated them against utter despair and propped up hopes for final victory. Their continued privileges also protected them from increased hardship on the home front. Yet nothing could disguise that certain Nazi leaders were heading for a fall. Hermann Goering remained the 'final court of appeal' in terms of the domestic economy and his economic empire expanded after Barbarossa.[5] However, his power base and standing with Hitler were eroded by the *Luftwaffe*'s failure to defend the Reich from bombs and the successful encroachment on his territory by rivals, to whom Hitler gave competing responsibilities. Goering watched helplessly, for example, as Hitler chose Albert Speer over him to be Minister of Armaments and War Production in February 1942.

Although Joseph Goebbels did not experience such an eclipse, he failed in his bid to have Hitler make him the dominant authority for mobilizing the *Volk* for 'total war'. Instead, Hitler appointed a 'Committee of Three' – Martin Bormann, Hans Lammers (head of the Reich Office of the Chancellor) and Field Marshal Wilhelm Keitel – to oversee the deployment of men and women to defend the Reich. They and other leading Nazis jockeyed for control, including the *Gauleiter* who did all they could to maintain their own power and popularity locally. The result was action without uniform goals and direction. Even the ever-devoted Goebbels recorded private frustrations with Hitler's leadership style, his growing distance from the German people, his refusal to discipline Party members for unbecoming conduct and his prioritization of military matters over the home front. Such frustrations, however, did not signal any weakening of the bond between Hitler and his leading political soldiers, a bond cemented by shared complicity in war and genocide.

Accomplices

Even after a decade of National Socialist rule, much remained of traditional societal structures. The conservative elites therefore retained a degree of power, privilege and authority over other Germans, distinct and yet inseparable from their capitulation to Nazi rule. This was particularly the case with German judges. In 1942, Hitler named himself Supreme High Justice. From this point, the *Führer* '*was* the law'.[6] Still, now as before, Hitler had no plans to dissolve the judicial system entirely. Under a new Justice Minister, Otto Thierack, and a newly appointed People's Court President,

Roland Freisler, it served Nazi purposes. First, it could be blamed for not doing enough to punish criminals, thereby excusing the police who were closely aligned to the National Socialist state. Second, the judiciary was critical to the Third Reich's purported commitment to the rule of law, however meaningless this veneer of legality was in practice. Most importantly, the courts had a vital role to play in Nazi terror, repressing political dissent and aiding the Nazis' assault on outsiders, especially the Jews. Justice Minister Thierack sent top-secret 'Judges Letters' as reminders to be ruthless in sentencing; as a result, 'normal' prisons held many more German inmates than the SS-run concentration camps did, at least until 1943. Judges handed down prison sentences more often than they ordered 'legal' executions, but those sentences did lengthen during the war, and were now given to defendants without prior criminal records, who previously received suspended sentences.

Hitler's top generals retained significant power over the men they commanded, at least in principle, even as they became little more than conduits of Hitler's orders. Initially, there was considerable confluence between their goals and strategies in the East and those of their Supreme Commander. Some had baulked at shifting the entire war effort to obliterating the Soviet Union but none objected very strenuously. They were resigned if not enthusiastic. Like Hitler, they totally misjudged the Red Army's size, strength and abilities. On 3 July 1941, General Franz Halder wrote, 'The Russian campaign has been won in the space of two weeks.' Just over a month later, on 11 August, he noted it had become 'increasingly plain that we have underestimated the Russian colossus.'[7] Even as winter descended, they nonetheless continued to believe that the Russian military was on the verge of collapse.

The military leadership generally shared Hitler's view that a war of annihilation had to play out along the Eastern Front and was complicit in barbarous crimes there. The generals themselves drafted the 6 June 1941 'Commissar Order' ordering the 'liquidation' of Soviet officials. The German Army was instrumental in the mass murders of civilians and prisoners of war just as it had been in Poland two years before. SS Special Task Forces perpetrated the majority of shootings by mutual agreement, but *Wehrmacht* officers on the ground also issued their own orders to deal with the population mercilessly.

Thus, the generals were not merely Hitler's puppets. Ideologically and strategically they were largely in agreement, even when, tactically speaking, they resented his interventions and had grave concerns about his assessment of military possibilities and German resources to realize them. There were other points of contention, including Hitler's prioritization of the southward drive to conquer the oil fields of the Caucasus and, in December 1941, the *Führer's* hard-line refusal to permit tactical retreats after the advance on Moscow stalled. Not surprisingly, the military elites expressed any disagreement extremely cautiously.

As the war progressed, Hitler sacked and replaced a number of leading generals and subordinate commanders who became scapegoats for his miscalculations. He increasingly preferred those of strong National Socialist convictions and personal loyalty who would accede to his ambitions and trust his genius and intuition. Cash payments and even great estates sweetened the pact between Hitler and some top officers, including General Heinz Guderian who travelled to Poland to choose the estate he wanted. Having tied themselves to a man who knew only two options – victory or annihilation – the military leaders had no viable alternatives themselves, other than stepping down. On 30 January 1943, Grand Admiral Erich Raeder resigned after another major German loss at sea, to be replaced by Karl Dönitz.

Big business' crimes against non-Germans and German outsiders mounted in these years. By continuing to pursue their own interests, while justifying their conduct as serving national ones, industrial elites made Nazi racial policy even more brutal. New ways of doing business became strikingly 'normal' as they chased profits and production targets. The Allianz insurance company wrote up policies for ghetto workshops and factories at concentration camps as if they were regular commercial enterprises. Corporations took over firms in the occupied territories themselves or entered into partnerships with the SS to run them. Moreover, German companies like Siemens, BMW and Volkswagen, to name only a few, opened factories at concentration camps; so too did Bayer, which also provided chemicals for human experimentation on prisoners. Degussa processed precious metals plundered from Jews. Topf and Sons designed and built camp crematoria ovens. Most notoriously, IG Farben sold Zyklon B to the SS; its upper management knew its purpose. Germany's largest companies were not alone in worsening – and ending – victims' lives. Even mid-level German shoe companies used prisoners on punishment details at Sachsenhausen to test the durability of their products.

Most of all, German enterprises, like German farms, benefitted from the toil of over eight million forced and slave labourers: prisoners of war, civilians from occupied countries, ghetto inhabitants and camp inmates.[8] Exploiting their labour was not only profitable, it was also essential. Without foreign workers, agricultural and industrial production likely would have collapsed by 1942. Companies paid exceedingly low wages for foreign forced labour and even less to the SS to 'lease' camp and ghetto inmates. Those slave workers received nothing at all. Believing Speer's assurances that there was still space for the entrepreneurial spirit, however much the Nazis dictated production priorities, industrialists extended work hours, intensified their pace and threatened punishment for poor performances to extract maximum profit. They also minimized expenditures on workers' food, housing and clothing. Business elites in the Third Reich were, as a group, willing to 'walk over corpses', a chilling German idiom meaning to stop at nothing.[9]

Dead and suffering bodies furthered the research agendas and careers of Germany's academic elites. The notorious Dr Josef Mengele became chief medical officer at Auschwitz in May 1943, selecting who lived or died on the arrival ramp. At other concentration camps, German scientists and doctors had been performing experiments on inmates for over a year, and even longer in the case of victims earmarked for 'euthanasia'. Research turned especially deadly in the service of the war effort. In Dachau, SS doctors observed the effects of hypothermia by plunging prisoners into icy water baths. At Ravensbrück, they inflicted, then infected, wounds on women known as 'rabbits' to investigate the effects of various drugs. Buchenwald inmates were deliberately burned with phosphorous. The fatality rate in human experimentation was high. Doctors and scientists also engaged in 'pure' research without any connection to the war,

Figure 4.1 Himmler (second from left) tours the IG Farben plant for producing synthetic rubber and liquid fuels under construction at Auschwitz, accompanied by the camp Commandant, Rudolf Höss (far right), and IG Farben personnel, July 1942 (Keystone/Getty Images).

like Mengele's own tests on identical twins at Auschwitz, 15 per cent of whom died because of them.[10] Medically trained 'euthanasia' personnel, already implicated in the murders of thousands, ensured many more died by advising on gassing techniques at Bełżec, Sobibór and Treblinka in spring 1942. Research scientists also benefitted from human 'material' even after death. One institute of neuropathology, thanking a paediatric hospital for recent specimens, ended by noting they were 'awaiting more brains!'[11]

Outside the medical field, university teaching became infinitely more challenging with the nation at war; academic research stagnated. Enlistment and conscription into war work affected student numbers. Publications in the arts and humanities became mere propaganda. Some among the traditional elites, including a few professors, now awoke to how thoroughly the Nazi state had violated their Christian, moral, conservative and/or nationalist values. Yet even as their experiences of the Third Reich in descent grew more terrible and terrifying, scarcely any acted against it in a meaningful way.

Supporters

A deteriorating military situation, intensified air raids, increasing repression and growing knowledge of atrocities shaped supporters' attitudes to the Nazi regime in this period. Conditions by the end of 1943 were scarcely imaginable as 1941 began. Despite relatively muted reactions to victories over Yugoslavia and Greece that year, Hitler's popularity was largely intact. His launch of Operation Barbarossa shocked most. Whether or not Germans believed Nazi propaganda that depicted it as a preventative action against 'Jewish-Bolshevism', the expansion of the war to two fronts triggered widespread fear. Rapid German advances within Soviet territory quickly reinvigorated admiration for, and loyalty to, the *Führer*. Morale dipped again with his declaration of war against the United States in December 1941, but its effect was blunted when no immediate consequences were felt at home. Of far greater concern were the signals following the stalled campaign outside Moscow. At the same time, surprisingly 'normal' routines and aspects of everyday life – marriage, childbirth, working life, even vacations – continued, especially in rural regions away from air raid danger. Goebbels's call for donations to the troops of winter clothing and even skis was worrying, but not all Germans followed his command to cancel their winter holidays.

There was even some good news, including initial successes by General Erwin Rommel's Africa Corps in Libya and German U-Boats in the north Atlantic. In 1942, though, doubts about the veracity of reports from the Eastern Front began to gain traction. The defeat at Stalingrad in early 1943 had dramatic consequences. Goebbels's inflammatory speech in February calling for radical 'total war' as the way to victory, though praised by the Propaganda Minister himself, had little positive effect on the population. The ranks of grieving widows and mothers grew. Fears of an unstoppable enemy mounted.

Figure 4.2 Hamburg after Operation Gomorrah air raids, July 1943 (Keystone/Getty Images).

Allied bombing – a formative experience on the home front – increased German sorrow and suffering; it also provoked resentment and distrust of the regime, which had failed to protect them. Major cities, from Bremen in the north to Munich in the south, experienced nightly air raids. A soldier home on leave, who experienced an attack in Cologne, noted it was 'better in Russia than here'.[12] The Hamburg firestorm in July 1943 was especially horrific. Operation Gomorrah, the most destructive series of raids on any German city, turned Hamburg into a giant oven. Flames killed thousands, as did the excessive heat, leaving 30–40,000 dead, 500,000 homeless and 50 per cent of the city destroyed.

Evacuees from urban centres and industrial regions now descended on rural villages in their thousands. Nazi organizations could not care for all displaced Germans in communal housing – repurposed hotels, guesthouses and schools – so adults and children were regularly billeted with locals. There was bitterness on both sides. City dwellers criticized country customs, dialects and meals. Children, missing their parents, misbehaved and wet their beds. Their hosts begrudged having to feed and care for those who refused to help with farm labour and looked down their noses at them. The vaunted *Volksgemeinschaft* certainly showed its cracks here.

Since 1933, supporters had separated their adulation for Hitler from their criticisms of Nazi Party bigwigs, whose corrupt, selfish actions the *Führer* supposedly knew nothing about. As Germany's military and home front situation deteriorated, more began to blame Hitler himself. The 'Heil Hitler' greeting grew less frequent. Some Catholics, when ordered to remove crucifixes, took down portraits of Hitler instead. Overall, Germans seemed to feel less angry at, than abandoned by, their *Führer*. Rare appearances on newsreels and infrequent radio speeches could not compensate for his physical absence. He never, unlike Goebbels, visited in the aftermath of an air raid. The Hitler Myth did not shatter between 1941 and 1943, but it did grow shakier.

Material conditions worsened for all Germans. Food shortages increased and prices rose. Many basic items were not available at all. Wives and mothers found it more difficult to care for their families, especially once the 1943 Law for the Defence of the Reich compelled women aged seventeen to forty-five into armaments production or other defensive work. Farmers, despite assistance from foreign labour, were exhausted, as were industrial workers, now commanded to produce even more. Small-business owners resented closures of their 'inessential' enterprises. The perceived link between sacrifices and victories had minimized grumbling in the first two years of the war. Now it grew.

Did an awareness of Nazi crimes affect wartime morale? Knowledge of the 'euthanasia' programs undeniably destroyed trust in Hitler for some Germans. Even after adult 'euthanasia' ended officially in 1941, public suspicions lingered. Transfers of patients to different locations and high patient death rates caused unease, destabilizing support for the regime. What supporters knew about the 'Final Solution' – in particular, the death camps themselves – will be addressed in Chapter 5, but information about massacres in the Soviet Union, the most intense phase of what is known as the 'Holocaust by bullets', definitely spread in some circles at home. Soldiers wrote surprisingly openly about the killings they witnessed or heard about, admitting the victims included women and children. However, the murders of Soviet Jews, which took place far away, did not ultimately sever the *Volk* from their *Führer*.

What then of Germans' responses to the plight of Jews from their own neighbourhoods? When the constellations of star-shaped badges appeared in September 1941, reactions ranged from surprise to disgust; most had no idea so many Jews remained in Germany. Indeed, their continued presence, highlighted by their sudden visibility, often aroused indignation when they dared to shop outside their allotted times. Antisemitic sentiment blaming them for daily wartime grievances increased. Although it is unclear whether most Germans actually believed Jews guilty of starting the war, as Hitler thundered, recent studies suggest that, by the end of 1943, belief in Allied bombing as retaliation for what Germans had done to the Jews was widespread.[13] As Jewish Germans disappeared – deported, gone underground or passing as 'Aryans' – there was some speculation about their fate, but daily concerns and personal suffering were pre-eminent. Individuals were undoubtedly sickened and horrified by what they learned or imagined; collectively, if they considered outsiders at all, it was usually only to wonder whether they might be next.

Some histories of the Third Reich at war emphasize the population's descent into despair and defeatism after Stalingrad and the firebombing of Hamburg. Others, more recently, cite evidence confirming high levels of broadly shared support for the regime even after those events. What is clear is that the German people did not now, and never did, rebel against the Nazi regime. Why? Ideological conviction was not the only, or even a key, motivator. Germans backed the Nazis for a variety of additional reasons, most of which also explain why they later committed to fighting to the very end. First, now more than ever, Germans were dependent on Nazi-run state and Party organizations for their very survival. The Nazi welfare organizations fed and sheltered those bombed out of their homes, the Nazi women's and youth organizations managed the evacuations of thousands of children from cities to the countryside, and SA men and other Party functionaries offered further assistance. This contributed to remarkable stability even after victories turned to ongoing setbacks.

Second, Nazi propaganda continued, despite the failures at Stalingrad, to boost hopes that Germany would prevail. The public's desperate desire to believe the regime's claims increased their effectiveness. Third, Germans continued to dream of future prosperity possible only with victory, while the new opportunities for profits, career advancement and self-actualization created by the expanded empire were worth fighting for in the present, as were the benefits of non-German labour at home. Fourth, unlike in the Great War and despite shortages, Germans were still reasonably well fed.

Several other considerations are important. Nazi terror played a substantial role in minimizing dissent, even though it remains debateable whether Germans supported the Third Reich primarily out of fear at this stage. It was certainly Himmler's intention that 'defeatists must die'.[14] The thoroughly Nazified judicial system awarded harsher sentences for an increasing array of infractions. Workers suffered more draconian punishments if they failed to meet production targets. Germans also backed this government in the belief that the 'stab in the back' of November 1918 must not happen again. To do otherwise, many felt – and the regime threatened – was treason. Finally, even as German supporters' patriotism, religious faith and longer-standing cultural traditions sustained their commitment to the war effort, whatever level of enthusiasm they felt about Nazism, there was a growing sense, propelled by Nazi propaganda, that only victory could stave off utter destruction. They saw no alternative. Desperate as they were for peace, therefore, their willingness to struggle on ensured that the final demise of Nazi Germany was still two years away.

According to Nazi ideology, the most violent struggle for German existence was playing on the frontlines of a racial war. 'Ordinary' supporters were active here too, notably in police battalions – with low rates of SS and even Nazi Party membership – that perpetrated mass shootings in the Soviet Union. Some policemen did ask to be spared the task and others claimed they deliberately missed their targets. Most asserted later, if asked, that they had merely followed orders, which they feared resisting, although there is no evidence that refusing to take part resulted in execution, severe punishment or even diminished career prospects. A potent combination of antisemitism, obedience, conformism and peer pressure explains their willingness to murder.

Female welfare workers and schoolteachers from the Old Reich were vitally important to another plank of the Nazis' racial project, the 'Germanization' of conquered lands in the East. With Slavs and Jews expelled, they worked to educate newly resettled ethnic Germans in housewifery, hygiene and child care, and contributed to the oppression of remaining non-German minorities. Women now served all branches of the *Wehrmacht* directly in greater numbers than before. Almost 400,000 German Red Cross nurses and nurses' aides and more than 500,000 female *Wehrmacht* auxiliaries, mostly typists, clerks and signalling assistants, were deployed to every theatre.[15] Thousands of women also took on aerial defence duties at home. Approximately half of these women volunteered. The other half, like male soldiers, had no choice.

Ten million German soldiers of the seventeen million who fought in the Second World War served on the Eastern Front. From all walks of life, they included ardent Nazis, supporters and even opponents of the regime. Most, like the military leadership, believed in the *Wehrmacht*'s superiority and doubted the Red Army's military effectiveness. Hopes for a swift victory rose during the first weeks of the campaign when they seemed on the verge of taking Leningrad, Kyiv and Moscow. 'It could not have been easier up to now', one soldier recorded in mid-July 1941.[16] Soldiers' attitudes to what would become millions of Russian prisoners of war hardened; their mass deaths in captivity stirred little pity. The civilians were filthy 'subhumans', their dwellings 'primitive': 'All they have here is pests and rubbish, not culture and civilization as we know it', noted a Catholic theology student.[17] As they travelled relentlessly eastwards, *Wehrmacht* soldiers observed and participated in the SS massacres of Soviet civilians. They also initiated their own.

Soldiers' initial exuberance masked the reality: the infantry's utter exhaustion after advancing dozens of kilometres per day, air crews' chronic difficulties with supplying a rapidly moving force, and casualties that, although lower *per diem* than during the Western offensive, continued day after day. Once the Russian winter

Figure 4.3 *Wehrmacht* soldiers shoot victims in Ukraine, *c*.1941 (Imagno/ Getty Images).

arrived – temperatures plunged to thirty degrees below – and the Red Army launched its counterattacks, German soldiers' real miseries began. Across Soviet territory, inadequately clothed and provisioned armies froze; in North Africa they sweltered under the blazing sun. By the end of 1942, German soldiers were dying for Hitler in astounding numbers from Stalingrad to Tunis as military setbacks climbed. Allied warships and planes were soon sinking one U-Boat per day, their crews often with them. Although some men began to question the meaning of such sacrifices, only very few chose to desert. They, like Germans on the home front, would defend Nazi Germany to the last.

Racial and social outsiders

The Nazis' murders of outsiders were well underway before the invasion of the Soviet Union. Thousands of disabled and 'asocial' Germans had already been 'euthanized'. Another secret program, Action 14f13, gassed concentration camp inmates unable to work. Deaths mounted in the concentration camps, juvenile prison camps and forced labour camps due to overwork, malnutrition, unhygienic living conditions and physical abuse. Court-ordered executions of wartime 'criminals', like alleged looters and black marketeers, skyrocketed. To have any chance for survival, outsiders had to prove their value as forced and slave labourers, under increasingly lethal conditions. Jewish Germans counted among all these categories of victims. Yet the short, intense wave of murders at the heart of the Holocaust was still to come. As late as March 1942, across Europe, an estimated 75–80 per cent of the Holocaust's eventual Jewish victims were alive; only eleven months later, in February 1943, only 20–25 per cent were.[18] The statistics for Sinti and Roma victims were similar.

An enormous academic literature describes the Nazis' deportations of Jews and Sinti and Roma from Greater Germany from autumn 1941, their arrival at the ghettos and camps in the East and the operations of the death camps where they met their end. This book cannot detail those horrors. No single experience was entirely typical, although there were shared features: terrifying days spent on overcrowded cattle trains

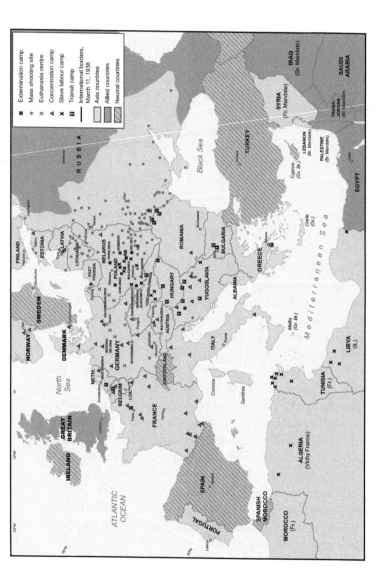

Map 5. Main Nazi extermination camps, mass shooting sites, 'euthanasia' centres, concentration camps, slave labour camps and transit camps across Europe and North Africa. (This redrawn map is based on one Facing History.org gave permission to reproduce.)

without food or water; the moment of selection for immediate death or temporary reprieve; undressing, delousing, shaving (and at Auschwitz, tattooing those spared for now); death by gassing or through back-breaking work; hunger and thirst; violent treatment and constant fear.

From 19 September 1941, Jews still in Germany, already segregated by a host of legal restrictions, were publicly marked by the obligation to wear a yellow Star of David on their clothing. Victor Klemperer, a former language professor living in Dresden, called that day 'the most difficult day in the twelve years of hell' he endured under the swastika.[19] Few dared to remove it and risk the concentration camp. Now immediately identifiable wherever they went, their life became hellish. They were vulnerable to public abuse, forbidden from buying most foods and other essential items and prohibited from travelling on public transportation, which added walking time to long hours of labour. Jewish workers always had to complete the most dangerous, dirty or disgusting tasks. When they heard the air raid sirens from their overcrowded 'Jew houses', they had nowhere to run; they were barred from public shelters. And always, the threat of deportation loomed. Some Jewish Germans decided to go into hiding or pass as 'Aryans', a brave and dangerous act of resistance described in the next section. Many more did not.

The Nazis assured Jews they were being sent 'only' to hard labour camps. What did Jewish Germans themselves know or believe of their eventual fate? Rumours naturally circulated, but without radios and relatives serving in the *Wehrmacht* or as occupation personnel in the East, and isolated from their better-informed 'Aryan' neighbours and contacts, they generally knew little. Moreover, sheer disbelief that genocide was a reality prevented most from acknowledging the possibility. Even when community leaders had accurate information about gassings in the death camps, some refused to share it so as not to force others to live in the expectation of death. As time passed, suspicions grew more widespread. As Jews prepared for imminent deportation, some were resigned to a horrible end that seemed almost preferable to unending horror.

Extermination also threatened the Nazis' other racial 'enemies'. The child 'euthanasia' programme never altered course, and actually grew

Figure 4.4 A Jewish woman with the Star of David badge, September 1941 (Sueddeutsche Zeitung Photo/Alamy Stock Photo/Scherl).

Figure 4.5 Watched by their neighbours, Jews are boarded onto the back of a truck during a deportation action from Kerpen, Germany, on 18 July 1942 (Courtesy of Stadtarchiv Kerpen, Bildarchiv Nr. 5830).

to include older children. Despite Hitler's official stop order in 1941, the murders of disabled and 'asocial' German adults entered a new 'wild' phase of decentralized killings, when victims' suffering ended not in gas chambers but in 'normal' hospital wards. Some died from injections, more from starvation, disease and neglect. To clear beds for wounded soldiers, Reich hospitals transferred ill patients with chronic medical conditions, like lung disease and diabetes, to 'rest homes' and 'recovery clinics'. Their estimated fatality rate was 75 per cent due to deliberate overdoses, abuse from medical staff, rampant infectious diseases, malnutrition and unsanitary facilities. Patients were often well aware of their fate. At Hadamar, in December 1942, one patient noted, 'more die here than on a battlefield.'[20] He was dead of a supposed heart attack three months later. The ability to work sometimes saved lives since it meant marginally better rations. Once those patients became too sick or dared insubordination, they too were murdered.

There was an additional route to possible survival for some racial and social outsiders: serving at the front. Although officially banned by the Nuremberg Laws from the *Wehrmacht*, some Black and Sinti Germans were nonetheless recruited as Nazi Germany's fortunes turned. For Hans Massaquoi, a Black German, the fact that the Armed Forces suddenly needed 'the likes of me' sent an obvious signal about a desperate situation.[21] The *Wehrmacht* also drafted some homosexuals interned in camps, making them serve in special punishment battalions. Though being sent to the frontlines was life-threatening, these gay men escaped the fate of others, who were executed at concentration camp work sites, killed in 'euthanasia' centres and laboured to death at stone quarries, brickworks and bomb disposal units.

Resisters

The year 1941 marked the revival of serious, political resistance to the Nazis with some important shifts in its source. First, those Germans once most likely to support the regime – young, Protestant, educated, middle-class, non-leftist insiders – took up oppositional activities in greater numbers. The best known of these were the members of the White Rose. This small group of Munich University students centred around two former HJ and BDM members, siblings Hans and Sophie Scholl. Hans had witnessed Nazi horrors first-hand while serving on the Eastern Front. In summer 1942, the group wrote and distributed five leaflets denouncing the Third Reich and its crimes. On 18 February 1943, a janitor observed Sophie scattering copies of their sixth leaflet in a university courtyard and contacted the *Gestapo*. Four days later, the People's Court found Sophie, her brother and an accomplice guilty of treason. They were beheaded by guillotine. Sophie was twenty-two. Their deaths failed to inspire the anti-Nazi riots they had hoped for; instead, Munich University students demonstrated in support of the regime.

Second, several still influential figures moved from religiously based dissent on specific issues to louder and more open criticism of the regime itself, which had a profound impact on Nazi policy.

In August 1941, Clemens August Graf von Galen, Catholic Bishop of Münster, gave an incendiary sermon condemning the murder of disabled Germans. It circulated throughout the country and was key to forcing Hitler's 'euthanasia' stop order that month. Reminding Catholics of the commandment 'Thou shalt not kill' and warning that even wounded soldiers might be at risk, Galen's words provoked deep unrest. Local Party leaders called for his execution. In fear of what his arrest might do to morale, the regime allowed Galen to remain in his pulpit. While such urgent, clear language about Nazi rule from a high-ranking clergyman was unparalleled, Galen nevertheless insisted the Catholic Church was no traitor seeking to overthrow the government. He did not raise his voice again when the deportations of Jews from Greater Germany began that autumn.

Third, previously isolated and often very diverse oppositional groups formed greater connections in this period. This greater potential for active resistance inflated the possibility of success, but also maximized chances of discovery by the *Gestapo*, which repeatedly outmanoeuvred and destroyed wider cooperative efforts. One of these more diverse groups, the Kreisau Circle (see Chapter 5), remained undetected, but a second, the Red Orchestra network, did not. This was an exceptionally motley mix of approximately 150 artists, middle-class intellectuals, Catholics, aristocrats, conservatives, pacifists and even some communists centred on Arvid Harnack, an advisor in the Economics Ministry, and Harro Schulze-Boysen, an official in the Aviation Ministry. The circle included an unusually high number of women, including Harnack's and Schulze-Boysen's wives. Active since the early days of Nazi Germany but now more numerous, these resisters drafted anti-Nazi leaflets, helped political opponents escape and informed American and Soviet embassies of Hitler's crimes. They also attempted to transmit details about the planned invasion of Russia using radios supplied by Soviet military intelligence. Radio traffic brought their activities to light in autumn 1942. Harnack, Schulze-Boysen, their wives and fifty other affiliates died by hanging at Hitler's personal insistence.

Finally, moral revulsion at antisemitic persecution either motivated more Germans to assist Jews for the first time or reconfirmed an existing commitment to oust the Nazis. For the plotters in the Military Intelligence Organization discussed in the previous chapter, it did both and was to be their undoing. The deportations of Jewish Germans deeply offended the Christian principles of the men around Hans Oster, including Protestant pastor Dietrich Bonhoeffer, as did reports of atrocities in the East. They began drawing up plans to smuggle Jews out of the country by earmarking them as indispensable to military intelligence. They also used police contacts to strike names off deportation lists. The *Gestapo* discovered the group's rescue efforts in April 1943. Oster was placed under house arrest. Bonhoeffer was sent to Berlin's Tegel Prison, and later, Flossenbürg concentration camp. For the time being, their roles in plotting Hitler's removal from power remained hidden, but Military Intelligence was no longer a locus of resistance.

These shifts aside, there were also important continuities in the story of German resistance. Numerically, communist resisters always predominated, though they neither approached the levels of 1933 to 1935 nor posed a genuine challenge to regime security. With Operation Barbarossa, they stepped up their illegal meetings, leaflet distribution and acts of sabotage. Otherwise, as before, private, individual actions by 'little' Germans – not coordinated endeavours by elites better placed to make a real difference – formed the bulk of oppositional efforts, especially those aimed at thwarting racial persecution. Arrests for the crime of being 'friendly to Jews', a direct challenge to regime commands, increased in this period. For example, some brave, lower-ranking priests and pastors, more Catholic than Protestant, now dared to pray publicly for Jews. Church leaders themselves largely refrained. Top-level resistance within the military also remained minimal, at least until the end of 1942. Plotters once committed to a coup saw Hitler's enduring popularity as a signal to hold off. The most significant continuity, of course, was in the tiny number of Germans willing to undertake *any* form of direct, active anti-Nazi activity at all.

To survive, outsiders had no choice but to keep thwarting the Nazis' intentions, but the horizon of possibilities for action grew ever narrower, the stakes never higher. Once deportations began, their fight continued in new locations across the continent alongside that of millions of non-German victims of Nazism. Those efforts to withstand and challenge persecution beyond the Old Reich were varied and courageous; our focus stays with the responses of those who remained in the heart of the Nazi empire.

One Jewish response to the threat of deportation was to hide. Diving as 'U-Boats', as it was called, demanded illegal activity, which prevented some law-abiding Germans from making that leap. Most hesitated for over a year after deportations began before submerging. Two-thirds of Jews who went into hiding – an estimated 12,000 (6,500 in Berlin alone) – likely did so only in the final months of 1942 and early 1943 in a desperate bid to survive.[22] Questions swirled: Where? For how long? And critically, who might help? The experience of Anne Frank, the best-known Jew in hiding, was not typical. She remained with her entire family in a single Amsterdam location, an annex with separate, full-height rooms, for two years, assisted by a core group of Dutch people they knew well, before being betrayed, deported to Auschwitz and dying at Bergen-Belsen. Far more common was moving, usually alone, from safe house to safe house, sometimes nightly, relying on a web of non-Jewish strangers, who could never be trusted entirely and who were themselves in constant danger. Without ration cards, Jewish hiders went hungry, as did their rescuers at times. 'U-Boats' worried about becoming ill and needing medical help. Some women suffered sexual abuse from those promising aid. They survived cramped, physically excruciating hiding spots in constant fear of detection to resist the Nazis' efforts to eliminate them.

Another possible way to survive involved 'passing' as 'Aryan', also illegal and thus intentionally anti-Nazi. This was easier for women than younger men, since most male Germans their age should have been serving on the front or at least be in uniform. Male bodies might also betray them, since Jewish men were circumcised and most 'Aryans' were not. Despite moving to cities with little chance of recognition, procuring false identification documents or disguising their appearance, it was impossible for some Jews to carry off the pretence. Their frightened demeanour and haunted eyes regularly gave them away. In the end, only a small percentage of hiders survived, whether by disappearing physically or camouflaging their real identities.

Jewish Germans temporarily protected by war work also opposed the Nazis. In May 1942, the Baum group carried out a daring arson attack on an anti-communist, antisemitic exhibition in Berlin ('The Soviet Paradise'), which injured eleven people. Herbert Baum was arrested at the Siemens factory. He died, probably by suicide, after extensive torture in prison. His wife, Marianne Baum, was executed for treason. Their actions unfortunately only drew attention to the remaining 40,000 or so Jews still in Berlin and reinvigorated Goebbels's drive to make the capital 'Jew free'.

Persecuted outsiders also challenged Nazi intentions through smaller, less dramatic – though no less defiant – choices. They sustained one another in the camps by sharing food, religious observances or workloads. They petitioned authorities for exemptions. They wrote letters to friends and family drawing attention to what was actually happening as they prepared for deportation or starved in a hospital ward. Communal relief efforts, now drastically reduced, still attempted to lessen suffering, at least until their leaders were deported, as in the case of the Reich Association for Jews in Germany in the latter half of 1943. Relatives of victims also protested on their behalf. The parents of a Viennese man arrested for homosexuality wrote to the Commandant of Flossenbürg concentration camp asking to visit him. Their concern may have saved his life. Parents complained to hospital directors about the starved appearance of their children, demanding their return home. In March 1943, during what became known as the Roses Street (*Rosenstrasse*) protest, several hundred 'Aryan' wives gathered outside a detention centre in Berlin where their Jewish husbands were being held, calling out support and trying to get food parcels to them.

Despite astounding courage, resilience and ingenuity, despite both selflessness and self-centred calculations, and even despite assistance from insiders, outsiders' exertions ultimately saved very few lives. Most often, it was sheer, almost unbelievable luck – not individual or collective efforts – that rescued them. Luck was to be in even shorter supply as the war dragged on.

CHAPTER 5
THE END (1944–1945)

The final eighteen months of Hitler's war were the bloodiest and most destructive of the entire conflict. Their magnitude and savagery are not easily described. They ended in apocalyptic ruin. Though the war in the West was clearly lost after the Allied invasion of Normandy, Northern France, on 6 June 1944 (D-Day), the Germans fought on. The Soviets' massive offensive launched later that month guaranteed a Red Army victory on the Eastern Front. It proved the deadliest defeat in German military history.

On 20 July 1944, Hitler survived an assassination attempt when a bomb planted by Army officer Claus von Stauffenberg exploded at the Wolf's Lair headquarters in East Prussia. Killing Hitler was to have been the first step of the plotters' game plan for a post-Nazi Germany (codenamed Operation Valkyrie), but a series of mishaps meant the coup quickly unravelled. Vicious retaliation against any suspected conspirators followed. It did not change Germany's military situation. By December 1944, virtually all of France, most of Belgium and part of the southern Netherlands had been liberated from Nazi domination. A newly formed People's Storm militia (*Volkssturm*), comprising young boys and old men, now faced the Allied forces drawing ever closer to Germany itself. In the West, the Americans crossed the Rhine River in March 1945. In the East, Soviet soldiers had liberated Auschwitz in January. By spring, they massed along the Oder River, forty miles from Berlin.

These were the most lethal months of the war. Over one million German soldiers died in 1945 alone, most on German soil. German refugees fleeing the Red Army died on their long treks. Allied bombs killed hundreds of thousands. The police, SS and military executed so-called malingerers and defeatists. German women, raped by Soviet soldiers, died of their wounds. The Nazis' most hated enemies – political opponents, Jews, Sinti and Roma, 'asocials', homosexuals and the disabled – were murdered or died of starvation, disease, neglect and torture in concentration camps, labour camps and hospitals, and on death marches criss-crossing Germany. Foreign workers and prisoners of war faced extermination through labour. Still German soldiers fought on and the home front did not disintegrate.

On 20 April 1945, Hitler's fifty-sixth birthday, the first Red Army units reached the outermost suburbs of the German capital. The Battle of Berlin commenced. On 30 April, having married his long-time mistress Eva Braun the day before, the *Führer* shot himself in the head. She ingested a cyanide capsule. The next day, Joseph and Magda Goebbels, who had moved into the Berlin bunker, poisoned their six children before killing themselves. The Nazi-led government based in Flensburg on the Danish border limped on under Hitler's successor, Grand Admiral Karl Dönitz, until Germany's final, unconditional surrender on 9 May 1945. While the Second World War did not end until Japan surrendered officially on 2 September 1945, the Third Reich was over.

Nazis

To the end, there were clear continuities in the dynamics of Nazism. The trends and trajectories noted in previous chapters – coordination and nazification, radicalization, escalation of terror and the centrality of the *Führer* himself – were always present. It was only now that the Third Reich came closest to the 'total state' its leaders had imagined; the Nazi Party's powers extended into every arena and snuffed out opposition ruthlessly. With an approaching German defeat, some leading Nazis lost their faith in National Socialism. Some even began to doubt Hitler himself. Yet since their power, careers and privileges derived solely from the regime itself, they had the greatest stake in continuing to support it. Their hands were also the dirtiest. Desperation to avoid capture motivated them, just as complicity in the worst Nazi crimes prompted acts of revenge against their victims, whom they blamed for endangering them. They had everything to lose.

By 1944, the Nazi Party was a mammoth organization of well over eight million members.[1] There was even an uptick in joiners that year, most of whom likely foresaw advancement opportunities as the Party tightened its grip on governmental organizations. Others sought to deflect suspicions about their loyalty, especially after the attempt on Hitler's life on 20 July 1944. Thousands of Nazi functionaries continued as full-time employees at all levels of the Party hierarchy. There was no clear pattern in how they responded to the final chaos. Some, sensing what was coming, discarded their uniforms, adopted new names and fled. Others slaved doggedly over Party work until the Allies arrived. Having increasingly assumed local and regional authorities' responsibilities, and fearful of punishment from their superiors, they were essential to controlling the German population, both insiders and outsiders.

Top-level Party functionaries remained consistently fanatical supporters of Hitler, at least outwardly. Only hardened, long-time National Socialists like themselves, they believed, could defend the Reich, even if victory itself was now unattainable. From 1 September 1944, the *Gauleiter* also gained increased power as Defence Commissars, a position previously held by some, but not all, of their number. In this role, they mobilized the People's Storm militia, convened court martials and threatened draconian measures against civilian 'defeatists'. The *Gauleiter* of Franconia, for example, threatened to burn villages raising white flags of surrender to the ground. Ultimately, only two of these forty-three Regional Leaders died fighting at their posts. The majority focused less on the fate of the Third Reich overall and more on events in their narrower realms. Individual ones even defied commands to hold out if they detected advantages to doing so.

The SS continued to inflict horrors on the inmates they guarded and marched across the Reich. They intensified their persecution of insiders too; anyone whose commitment to repelling the Allied onslaught was suspect. Especially fanatical SS men and other Nazi Party functionaries formed 'Werewolf' and 'Freikorps "Adolf Hitler"' units. Their partisan-style, guerrilla-type tactics had no real effect on Allied armies – they were poorly led and armed, and did not have popular support – but they did murder thousands, including German civilians, and inflicted extensive property damage. In Aachen, they assassinated the American-appointed mayor. In these crimes of the last hour, older Stormtroopers and younger Hitler Youth ably assisted SS fanatics.

Why did these Nazis keep on killing? Certainly genuine commitment to the Nazi world view, which demonized racial enemies, played some part, alongside a determination to punish 'traitors' to avoid another revolution like the one in November 1918. Revenge fuelled murder as well, revenge against those seen as having spoiled their dreams of a purified, dominant *Volksgemeinschaft*. Like their *Führer*, these Nazis had long ago burned their bridges.

The key Nazi leaders in this period, apart from Hitler of course, were Himmler, Goebbels, Bormann and Speer. The first two had played pivotal roles in the Third Reich since 1933; the influence of the others became more crucial only recently. After the assassination attempt of July 1944, an event that dramatically radicalized the Nazi regime, all four enjoyed more authority than ever before and steered the regime's course during its death throes. Goebbels finally gained long-sought extensive powers over many sectors of public life as Reich Plenipotentiary for Total War. Himmler was granted considerable military clout, especially as Commander-in-Chief of the Reserve Army, and even more importantly, an almost total 'monopoly over the means of coercion within the Reich'.[2] Bormann was tasked with overseeing the Nazi Party, while Speer supervised the war economy, including forced labour. These men – the truest of the true believers – reaped the benefits of loyalty to Hitler even as they continued to war with one another. Other players, like Goering, fell from grace. Yet within their own fiefdoms, enduring influence further complicated the structures of Nazi governance.

Throughout 1944 and early 1945, Hitler's henchmen seemed to share his 'all or nothing' mentality. Speer was more realistic than the others were, but he could see no alternative to maximizing industry's contribution to the war effort. By early 1945, though, even Goebbels, the only Nazi leader committed to dying with the *Führer* in the bunker, advocated a political settlement with Stalin. Bormann too considered negotiating with Marshal Georgy Zhukov, the Soviet general who later received the German unconditional surrender. Himmler reached out secretly to the Western Allies to negotiate Jewish prisoner releases and propose an anti-Soviet alliance. Shocked and outraged at that imagining of a post-Third Reich future, on the day before he killed himself, Hitler ordered Himmler's arrest. In the final moments, then, these most fanatical Nazis could not accept Hitler's either/or vision completely.

Despite the authority wielded by these four men, Hitler's power remained absolute throughout 1944 and into 1945. He was 'head of state, commander-in-chief of the armed forces, head of government and head of the Party'.[3] As long as he was alive, the war would continue. His dichotomous vision – victory or annihilation – never wavered, and he claimed victory was still possible. Surviving the assassination attempt boosted his paranoia, but it also buoyed his sense of a divine mission. He felt invincible. In the rare moments when he acknowledged Germany's predicament, he indicated a plan to go down fighting rather than capitulate, revealing his commitment to national destruction if the war could not be won. Physically, however, the war years had taken their toll. He suffered a minor heart attack in September 1944, and the symptoms of what was likely Parkinson's disease – trembling limbs and muscle weakness – grew more pronounced. He developed stomach cramps, jaundice and polyps on his vocal chords. The medications prescribed by his attending physicians likely worsened his health. He kept his physical deterioration hidden from the German people. Long before he descended to his bunker below Berlin, he had largely disappeared from public view.

What sustained Hitler's irrational optimism, or at least what he projected externally? He believed his V1 and V2 'wonder weapons' (newly developed flying bombs) would strike sufficient terror to bring Allied air raids to an end; a new Ardennes offensive would repeat the glorious events of spring 1940, while success in the West freed up troops to halt the Soviet advance; the strange Allied partnership between communists and capitalists would splinter; and the total

Figure 5.1 Hitler with Hitler Youth members on his fifty-sixth birthday, 20 April 1945, ten days before he committed suicide in his bunker below Berlin (Popperfoto via Getty Images/Getty Images).

mobilization of the home front would enable a final push. Like his role model, Prussian king Frederick the Great, Hitler would snatch victory over the Russians from the jaws of defeat. Only in late April 1945 did he finally admit, explicitly, that the war was lost. Capitulation was not an option for Hitler. He vowed not to suffer public humiliation as had his ally, Benito Mussolini, his corpse hung upside down in a Milan square, spat on and stoned by onlookers. Instead, Hitler's self-proclaimed heroic end was suicide. There was to be, quite literally, no life after the Third Reich. Other leading Nazis, though definitely not all, followed his example; so too did scores of 'ordinary' Party members in the final weeks of the war and those immediately following its conclusion.

Accomplices

With the punishing Allied invasion of France in summer 1944, the failure of the *Wehrmacht*'s final offensive through the Ardennes and the Soviet push westward in early 1945, the German traditional elites recognized the war was lost. Certain individuals maintained limited power to end the frontline fighting and stop the violence exploding across the Reich; most felt unable to change these circumstances and so it continued. Just as these elites helped bring Hitler to power, so too they helped prop up his regime until the final collapse. Some did so out of a sense of duty to the state and the nation, others out of an enduring loyalty to the *Führer*. Only his death severed that bond.

Professors' teaching and research careers were mostly on hold. By July 1944, bombing raids had severely damaged over one-third of higher education institutions in the Greater German Reich. University education essentially ended that year apart from disciplines considered vital to the war effort; however, German scientists carried out mass sterilization experiments on female prisoners at Auschwitz almost until the Red Army was at the gates. Medical professionals continued to kill in other ways too by selecting deportees for extermination at the camps and 'euthanizing' hospital patients, camp inmates and foreign labourers unable to work. Germany's academic elites never turned against Hitler en masse. Few could envisage a post-Hitler world. Even those who did, like Gerhard Ritter, a well-respected historian imprisoned as part of the plot to kill Hitler, clung to a vision of an authoritarian form of government.

The Nazi regime maintained the facade of an operating legal system until the war's final days, though in practice, the *Gestapo* exacted 'justice' far more frequently. *Gestapo* officers sent individuals to camps or shot them outright without even the most cursory judicial process. On-the-spot executions of 'criminals', such as looters and so-called defeatists, were commonplace, especially if these were foreign workers. At the same time, German judges contributed substantially to the orgy of violence that marked these last months. The People's Court sentenced thousands to death in the wake of the assassination attempt in July 1944, for example. The Special Emergency Tribunals rendered judicial autonomy even more farcical. Justice Minister Thierack created these summary court martials at Himmler's behest in February 1945. They hauled in soldiers and civilians accused of 'disintegrating' resolve to fight on. If found guilty, of desertion or hanging out a white flag of surrender, a triad of a criminal court judge, a Nazi Party official, and a *Wehrmacht*, Waffen SS or police officer, sentenced them to death immediately: an estimated 6,000–7,000 died as a result.[4] The court martials typified the symbiotic relationship between German judges and Nazi 'justice', a hallmark of the Third Reich, which persisted, unchallenged, to the end.

The government ministries kept running with skeletal staffs once high government officials fled Berlin in early spring 1945. Central administration disappeared, but, honour-bound to the state, civil servants held meetings, filed reports, sent memoranda and ensured salaries were paid. They bore responsibility for allowing Nazi Germany to go on by making the bureaucracy function as well as possible.

As defeat became inevitable, Germany's business elites grew more, not less, determined to wring all they could out of millions of forced and slave labourers. Labour camps proliferated even as military setbacks accumulated. In ever more horrific and exploitative conditions, forced workers had to transfer machinery underground, safe for a post-war revival, and keep essential plants operating so that company owners might avoid frontline duty. Time and materials were to be saved at the cost of sufficiently feeding and housing their coerced labour force. Until mid-1944, when Allied bombing reversed the trajectory, war production of all major weapons continued to increase under Speer. The industrialists cooperated well with him, since their desire to protect their facilities generally matched his. They also shared Speer's concerns about advancing SS inroads into the war economy; that did not impede working with the latter to remove camp inmates from factories as the Allied troops arrived to present a 'cleaner' image. The business elites' cynical, self-centred opportunism knew no bounds. They had contributed enormously to Nazi Germany's ability to fight on long after the war was lost. Now they pivoted easily, ready to help the Allies rebuild their shattered country.

The assassination attempt on Hitler in July 1944 usually dominates the story of German military elites in this period. While the plotters' courage must be recognized, such an emphasis threatens to camouflage important realities. First, they were an extremely small and isolated minority, and, on the whole, only mid-ranking officers. The vast majority of the German field marshals, generals and admirals remained supportive of the Nazi regime and deeply loyal to Hitler as their Supreme Commander. They considered the plotters to be unpatriotic traitors who had severely endangered the war effort. Second, unlike the conspirators, who all thought Hitler's assessments of, and prognoses for, the military situation were completely mistaken, the majority adopted some version of Hitler's position. This itself made collective, widespread action by the German military leadership against him impossible. Openly disparaging the *Führer*'s calculations risked dismissal – Hitler did not execute or imprison the men whom he felt failed him on the frontlines – but even in the hands of their Allied captors after the war, when there were no negative consequences for doing so, few generals initially criticized his military decisions.

Third, focus on the conspiracy overshadows not only the military elites' disregard for suffering German civilians – they cared far more about protecting their men and material – but also, in retreat, their continued complicity in crimes against citizens of enemy countries, and, increasingly, against fellow German citizens. The top ranks of the military hierarchy were well aware of the 'Final Solution' and the role their own troops played in mass murder. That knowledge did not hinder the majority's dedication to the war in Hitler's name. No longer fighting for victory, or indeed any concrete strategic goals, they committed only to defending the Reich, while buying time, hoping something might alter the course of events. In the process, their measures against both their own soldiers and German civilians became more repressive. In the final months of the war, *Wehrmacht* leaders and Waffen SS officers alike ordered summary executions of defeatists, saboteurs and anyone daring to negotiate with Allied forces.

The German military elites were indispensable to prolonging the life of the dying regime and thereby prolonging human loss and the destruction of Germany. The ten months of fighting after 20 July 1944 – the date of the attempt on Hitler's life – killed more Germans and destroyed more German cities than did the first five years of the war combined. As the chain of command broke down amidst the chaos, individual officers increasingly acted on their own initiative.

Some bravely disobeyed the call to hold out, thereby saving towns and lives, but risking SS retribution in the process. Others chose to inflict terror themselves, turning a brutal war even more savage. Most simply persisted to the best of their ability in the fulfilment of their duty, to country and *Führer*, to the final unconditional surrender.

Supporters

It is impossible to generalize about 'all' or even 'most' supporters' responses from 1944 to 1945 beyond an almost universal desire for the horrors of war to end. Attitudes ran the full spectrum from genuine belief in a final victory to fatalistic dread of inevitable annihilation. Reactions too ranged from desperate refusals to give up the fight to acts of disobedience aimed at ending hostilities. Popular faith in Hitler was in free fall by early 1945 – barring some exceptions, more commonly among youth schooled in Nazism – when only six months before the majority of Germans seemingly had difficulty imagining a post-Hitler future. The popular response to his surviving the plot against him had overwhelmingly been authentic relief. 'What would we have done without the *Führer*?' people asked.[5] Many were profoundly indignant and angry: at the plotters, the *Wehrmacht* as an institution and the Nazis for not discovering their treachery earlier. Thereafter, support for Hitler played an increasingly minimal role in motivating Germans to struggle on. Intensely war weary, terrified of Soviet occupation, feeling helpless to alter events and driven by a sense of duty to the nation, supporters never rebelled collectively, even when morale was at its lowest ebb.

Massive property damage and dislocation broke down certain societal divisions between supporters, albeit in ways the regime had not intended. As the war came home, civilians and soldiers alike witnessed, took part, and died in combat. Air raid shelters brought together young and old, men and women, rich and poor, while excluding Jews, foreign workers and other outsiders. Locals and newly arrived refugees and evacuees of diverse professional, religious and regional backgrounds cowered in the dark together. Yet the commonalities in experience should not be overstated. Gender, class, background and other societal factors differentiated Germans from one another to the end. So too did location. By 1945, Germans increasingly sought to defend neither the Reich nor the *Volk*, but their own town or village from destruction. How that played out varied enormously across the country. In the West, the Allies, especially Americans, were often greeted with enthusiasm; in the East, fears of Soviet communism and Red Army vengeance, fuelled by Nazi propaganda and refugees' tales of atrocities, motivated more tenacious holding out. The breakdown of central authority made these circumstances unavoidable; however, they also revealed that the Nazis' imagined *Volksgemeinschaft* – wherein racially defined equals committed to a national cause over and above anything else – had failed to supplant traditional loyalties and individual interest.

German suffering increased exponentially. First, there was massive uprooting and displacement. The refugee treks by ethnic Germans fleeing Red Army advances were agonizing due to freezing conditions, Soviet vengeance and Party repression demanding People's Storm 'volunteers'. Thousands perished. Evacuations from the West could be similarly chaotic and frightening, since Party functionaries often approved them just as the Allies arrived.

Second, in the very last weeks of the war, 'Aryan' Germans lost contact with, and knowledge of the whereabouts of, their loved ones. Until then, however, they had benefitted from a well-functioning communication system that facilitated letters to and from the front and correspondence between children in rural evacuee camps and their parents. A Berlin couple on holiday in Upper Silesia even mailed a postcard – dated 20 July 1944 – rating their trip as a 'very nice tour'.[6] Other pockets of 'normality' were similarly astonishing. Germans went to their offices and showed up on factory assembly lines until they were bombed; they visited the cinemas until they were closed; they read newspapers and even attended football games until those also ceased.

Third, more supporters than ever before – men, women and children – were forced to labour for the Reich, as armaments workers, trench and fortification builders, and aerial defence auxiliaries under exhausting, dangerous and frightening conditions. Fourth, 'Aryan' women now suffered mass sexualized violence. Red Army soldiers raped hundreds of thousands of women as they advanced through eastern Germany and into Berlin. Some women died from the effects of the brutal, repeated assaults or took their own lives in shame.

Fifth, in greater numbers, insiders now experienced Nazi terror. 'Slacking' on the job was equated with military desertion; both 'crimes' could earn the death penalty. 'Defeatism' – expressing pessimism or hanging out a white flag of surrender – could get Germans killed. Corpses hanging from improvised gallows served as effective reminders. Police and Waffen SS officers, and sometimes even regular *Wehrmacht* soldiers, murdered hundreds in the unchecked violence that marred the final weeks of the war. Fear and coercion were thus undoubtedly significant in Germans' continued support of the war effort. Any sign of dissent was risky, but even riskier for those who had a history of oppositional views. The regime intended that no one who had wished for the Third Reich's demise might survive to glory in its death. Yet, unlike racial and social outsiders, whose very survival hinged on defying the regime's intentions, insiders' survival usually depended on compliance with its aims and commands. Resistance and disobedience were exceedingly rare, right to the end.

Despite the inevitability of defeat and the consequences of continuing the war for the civilian population, German soldiers, sailors and airmen overwhelmingly fought loyally to the end. Why? Historians offer several explanations. Some were motivated by genuine identification with Nazi values and fanatical faith in the *Führer*; the Nazis' increased indoctrination efforts after July 1944 likely strengthened or reinvigorated these. A simpler refusal to break the oath they had sworn inspired others. Obedience and loyalty thus merged with patriotism, soldiers' desire to protect their country and a commitment not to abandon their comrades. There was also fear: fear of reprisals against themselves and their families for desertion, fear of Red Army revenge should they be taken prisoner and fear of what Soviet occupation might mean for their loved ones. Fear of falling into Anglo-American hands was usually less widespread. Despite those fears, approximately 35,000 German soldiers were sentenced for

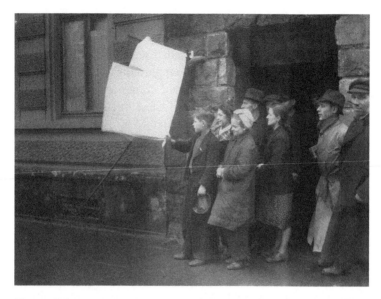

Figure 5.2 Germans in the city of Monchengladbach with white flags of surrender, April 1945 (Fred Ramage/Getty Images).

desertion and 15,000 executed.[7] Unknown numbers avoided service, either accidentally or intentionally, when they became separated from their units in the final chaos. The vast majority, however, fought on, if not for Hitler then for the homeland.

Increasingly raw recruits now joined them on the frontlines: young male teenagers and those whose fitness levels were less than ideal. Goebbels had 'combed out' the latter from various sectors of the economy, like the cultural and entertainment sectors. Truly able-bodied men largely remained at work in exempted armaments factories. While fifteen- and sixteen-year-olds were given more extensive military training, the older and less physically fit men were treated as cannon fodder with two weeks or less to learn the basics. Boys and older men also defended the home front in the People's Storm militia. Some served it willingly, while others tried to gain exemptions, rarely successfully. Only a fraction ended up in actual combat; instead, some used their weapons to guard camp inmates and enforce security measures after air attacks, threatening or even shooting suspected looters. They too aided the Nazi repression apparatus, propping up the Third Reich and prolonging its death throes.

To the very last, then, German supporters facilitated – and at times directly perpetrated – abuse and crimes against those who, by choice or by their very existence, defied the Nazis' totalitarian ambitions. In one town, for example, a crowd of 'ordinary' Germans punched and kicked a teenager caught distributing leaflets urging surrender before the hangman placed the noose around his neck. The Americans arrived four hours later. Elsewhere, Germans denounced others for listening to enemy radio broadcasts or uttering defeatist statements. As always, however, outsiders suffered most from insiders' indifference and active persecution. When the emaciated, sickly and weak camp inmates marched through their towns, Germans reacted with fear and revulsion. They must be real criminals, they told one another, to be punished like that. They threw stones, spat or verbally abused them. Many more looked away, ignoring pleas for water or bread. Exceedingly few did anything to help.

The death marches made the Nazi regime's treatment of outsiders, Jews in particular, more visible and contributed to Germans' changing knowledge of the Holocaust in these years. When the front arrived on their doorstep, so did more concrete information about the camps, including the death camps. As prisoner numbers rose throughout the war, more Germans, as policemen, administrative officials and railway workers, came into direct contact with them. Additionally, as the coerced workforce grew, their wretched condition became more conspicuous. There were other clues too. Deportations from the Reich took place in full public view while rumours and discussion about mass shootings in the East were commonplace. As Jewish Germans disappeared, so too did the anti-Jewish signs. It was clear to anyone who wanted to piece things together that they were not returning. An example of how extensive such knowledge was, and how cavalierly it was shared, shows up in the comment of a woman fleeing the eastern city of Breslau in January 1945. Seeing prisoners in striped uniforms at the train station, her fellow refugees wondered if they might be Jews. She dismissed such speculations: 'They have all been shot in Poland already.'[8]

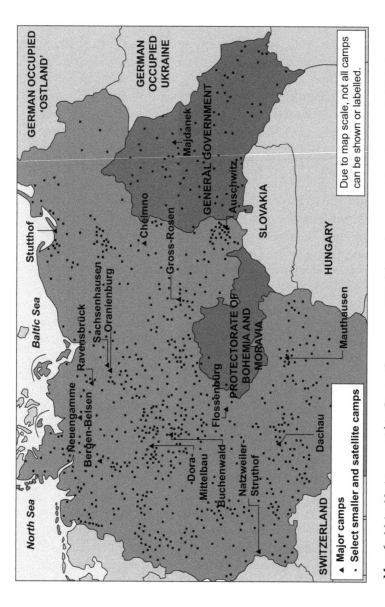

Map 6. Major Nazi camps within Greater Germany in 1944. (This redrawn map is based on one the United States Holocaust Memorial Museum gave permission to reproduce.)

Most Germans later maintained they only learned about the gas chambers after the war. Certainly, the true scale and scope of the extermination of European Jews emerged post-war, but evidence suggests information about the 'Final Solution' circulated long before that. In autumn 1942, for example, a German private on his way to the front penned a letter home from the town of Auschwitz: 'The Jews arrive here … at a weekly rate of 7 to 8,000; shortly thereafter, they die a heroes' [sic] death.'[9] Being confronted with evidence of Nazi crimes was, of course, different from trusting it. Even those sympathetic to Jewish Germans, including one woman risking her life to hide them, asked, when faced with credible sources about Auschwitz-Birkenau, 'Is one to believe such a ghastly story?'[10] Some Germans must have tried to make sense of what they were hearing. Many more likely paid it little attention, far more concerned with their own personal situations. Only the revenge the Jews might exact troubled them, which in itself suggests Germans knew there was cause for retribution.

In the final weeks of the war, thousands of 'Aryan' Germans committed suicide, over 3,800 in Berlin alone.[11] In choosing to take their own lives, they shared an experience that was outwardly analogous to that of some Nazi victims. However, the timing and motivations were poles apart. When Nazism had seemed unstoppable, some outsiders saw dying as the only alternative. In this, they defied the regime power over their life and death. By contrast, insiders killed themselves only once Nazi Germany's destruction was assured, propelled by fear of Allied victory and despair at a world without Hitler.

Racial and social outsiders

The final years of the war both sharpened and blurred definitions of who belonged to the *Volksgemeinschaft* and who did not. The Nazis' definition remained consistent even as they punished 'racial comrades' for purportedly acting against the *Volk*'s interests. Supporters, though, now viewed a new group as outsiders and a source of considerable tensions: millions of ethnic German refugees from Poland, Hungary, Romania and Yugoslavia, who fled the Red Army's advance from autumn 1944 onwards. Reich Germans resented having to share already limited food and housing with these unwelcome arrivals. The refugees themselves recall being treated as inferiors despite Nazi propaganda touting their racial equality.[12]

Their suffering, however genuine, did not compare, in severity, scope or duration, to that of regime-defined outsiders. The Third Reich maintained its capacity for terror and violence against them until the very end, long after Auschwitz-Birkenau and the other death camps ceased gassing operations in late 1944 and early 1945. The litany of miseries was unimaginably horrific. For camp inmates, foreign workers, prisoners of war and hospital patients, starvation – long a threat – loomed even larger, labour became more lethal, air raids were deadlier for them and arbitrary punishment and murder grew more likely. At the same time, the death marches became a new murderous torment to withstand. These forced evacuations of the concentration camps in the East, the largest from Auschwitz, began in winter 1944/1945.

The ostensible aims of the marches were threefold: to prevent prisoners falling into Allied hands as living evidence of Nazi crimes; to preserve a remnant labour force for the armaments industry; and, for Himmler, to retain a possible bargaining chip in negotiations with the Allies. Hundreds of thousands of prisoners had to walk huge distances to camps in the Reich's interior, or ride in freight trains exposed to the elements. One-third to one-half were Jews.[13] The brutality of SS guards accompanying them was stunning; SA guards were rarely kinder. Those who could not keep up, or who dared any insubordination, were shot. In one case near Magdeburg, guards – with assistance from Hitler Youth boys, Labour Service recruits, soldiers and local Nazi Party functionaries – locked over one thousand prisoners into a barn and set it alight rather than continue the journey. Marchers received little, if any, food or drink, died from exposure to freezing winter temperatures and endured verbal abuse from witnesses. Should anyone try to escape, Hitler Youth, soldiers stationed nearby and local citizens joined in the hunt. The marches continued as the SS repeatedly moved prisoners to camps deeper within Germany. Regular prisons were now 'evacuated' as well, although authorities often killed Jews and those found guilty of the most severe 'crimes' before departure. Prisoners criss-crossed the country almost to the last day of the war. The camps they arrived at offered no respite. They were hellishly overcrowded, poorly provisioned and disease-ridden. Their SS guards became more brutal the closer Nazi Germany's collapse came.

Resisters

Only a small number of Germans ever actively and intentionally resisted Hitler, some from the earliest days of his dictatorship, others only now as an end lay in sight. None of their efforts succeeded in bringing down the Nazi regime. Only military defeat by non-Germans achieved that. Ironically, the best-known plot that came closest to killing the *Führer* only made things worse in terms of an escalation of terror. By contrast, less dramatic moments of disobedience by nameless insiders sometimes managed to bring peace locally, if not to the country as a whole, thereby preventing further destruction and saving lives. A few brave rescuers and helpers assisted Jews, who, along with other outsiders, carried on their own struggle to outlast the Third Reich.

The 20 July 1944 assassination attempt had significant repercussions for the *Wehrmacht*, German insiders and Hitler himself. The conspirators were united in a desire to remove the *Führer* from power and restore the 'full majesty of the law', as they put it, but they differed greatly over what Germany might look like without him.[14] Claus von Stauffenberg, who detonated the bomb in the Wolf's Lair headquarters, was a devout Catholic from an aristocratic family who had initially sympathized with Nazism. He was severely wounded serving in North Africa, losing an eye, a hand and three fingers on the other. Horrified by the atrocities on the Eastern Front and convinced Hitler's military gambles would lose the war, he committed to killing him. As the new Chief of Staff for the Reserve Army, he had direct access. Stauffenberg, who was originally closer to Carl Goerdeler and Ludwig Beck, older leaders of the conservative opposition, opened up more to the ideas of younger men connected to his cousin, Peter Yorck von Wartenburg, and the so-called Kreisau Circle who met at Helmuth

James von Moltke's estate in Upper Silesia. These men, both from well-known Prussian military families, shared a profound disgust at Nazi antisemitism. They gathered other aristocrats, civil servants, socialists and clergymen to discuss regime change founded on more progressive principles. They also planned to punish Nazis for their crimes.

Van Moltke had already been arrested in January 1944. Kreisau Circle members who had tried to contact the communist underground soon followed. Operation Valkyrie – the scheme for loyal Army troops to occupy Berlin after Hitler's death and arrest Nazi leaders there and at other strategic European locations – came to nought. Stauffenberg was among the first of the conspirators to die by firing squad. Beck and other military officers committed suicide. More than a hundred more, including relatives of suspected plotters, were arrested, tried by the People's Court and executed, some hanged gruesomely from meat hooks in Berlin's Plötzensee Prison, filmed for Hitler's viewing pleasure. Goerdeler was sent to prison, where, in 1945 he was killed, along with Moltke, Oster and Bonhoeffer, men who had also conspired against Hitler. Had the plot been successful, it would have stopped the war and mass murder, saving hundreds of thousands of lives.

While the conspiracy had failed, in the final weeks of the war, 'ordinary' insiders did save lives by disobeying Hitler's command to fight to the end. Individual houses and sometimes entire villages hung out white flags of surrender, teenagers circulated leaflets calling for peace and women demonstrated publicly, urging German troops to lay down their weapons. Some civic officials tried to make contact with the Allies themselves. Partisan-type activity against the *Wehrmacht*, including sabotage, was rare, but did occur. Austrian communists assisted the Red Army as it entered Vienna. Elsewhere in the Reich, the members of the National Committee Free Germany, a German resistance group based in the Soviet Union, stood poised to take over in the Soviet-occupied zone. There was no mass public uprising, but in certain locations, the war ended earlier because Germans finally took a stand against the Nazis.

Other Germans opposed them by helping Jews: providing food, ration stamps, accommodation and false papers for their life in hiding. What motivated them to commit the crime of what the regime called being 'friendly to Jews'? Some, like those in the Socialist Bund group in Düsseldorf, had strong anti-Nazi political sympathies. Catholic and Protestant clergy and laity acted out of Christian convictions. Humanitarian compassion moved others, such as the 'Uncle Emil' network in Berlin created by the journalist Ruth Andreas-Friedrich and her husband, an orchestra conductor. Still others cynically realized that rescuing Jews might deflect from their prior complicity with the Nazis, explaining why even SA men were among those who fed Jews in hiding.

In the war's final stages, Germans suddenly found themselves confronted by new situations, such as when they encountered escapees from concentration camps or death marches, where their actions meant life or death for another human being. At risk to themselves, some chose to help. Those risks were sizable, ranging from fines to incarceration. Yet, there was no officially proscribed punishment for Germans helping Jews. By contrast, Poles under Nazi occupation faced the death penalty for coming to their assistance.

Some rescuers became well-known after the war, like Oskar Schindler, the Sudeten German who saved Jews by employing them in his enamelware factory in Cracow. The vast majority remain invisible to history, but they were always hugely fewer than those who perpetrated crimes against Jews or did nothing to stop them. What did these rescuers have in common? All research points to the same conclusion: the only thing they shared was a willingness to risk themselves to help Jews, even those unknown to them personally. Yad Vashem, the World Holocaust Remembrance Center, honours individual Germans who rescued Jews as 'Righteous amongst the Nations'. It notes that, 'in their broad spectrum of differing social origins, religious beliefs, political affiliations and occupations they appear to constitute a veritable cross-section of German society: housewives, soldiers, laborers, industrialists, artists, medical doctors, scientists, peasants, city dwellers, country folk, clergymen, nuns, atheists, lesbians, conservatives, communists, social democrats' and more.[15]

To survive Hitler, German outsiders were often dependent on insiders, but their own actions were also instrumental: entering the air raid shelter clutching false papers; escaping a death march; enduring another night in hiding; withstanding another day's labour; helping others like themselves. All German victims of National Socialism alive when the war ended had thwarted the regime's aims. The millions of outsiders who had not survived, essentially because so few other Germans had resisted the Third Reich, live on every time we tell their stories of resilience, defiance, perseverance and generosity. In honouring their memory, we also spoil the Nazis' intentions that it be obliterated.

CONCLUSION: COMING TO TERMS WITH NAZI GERMANY

The Third Reich began in flames and ended in ashes. By May 1945, roughly seven million Germans were dead. They died on the battlefield and under the bombs; they were starved and murdered in prisons, camps, hospitals, ghettos, killing fields and gas chambers. Cities and towns were reduced to rubble. Millions were homeless and millions were not where they wanted to be. At one time, areas under Nazi Germany's control or influence encompassed nearly all of Europe and beyond, stretching from the English Channel to the outskirts of Moscow, from the Arctic Circle to the coast of North Africa. Now the United States, France, Great Britain and the Soviet Union directly occupied the former German Reich. Hitler, Goebbels, Bormann and Himmler were dead. The Allies brought Goering, other Nazi functionaries and their accomplices to trial at Nuremberg, though Goering killed himself before his death sentence was carried out. Men like Ribbentrop and Keitel were executed. Speer, Dönitz and Women's Leader Gertrud Scholtz-Klink were imprisoned. Others, such as Adolf Eichmann, escaped punishment for decades by fleeing abroad. The vast majority of Germans who survived the Third Reich paid no penalty for their role in supporting it. Those cast outside the imagined *Volksgemeinschaft* never fully escaped the legacy of unimaginable suffering.

Since 1945, historians have argued about what exactly Nazi Germany was. Was National Socialism a form of totalitarianism, a type of fascism, an extreme variety of authoritarian populism or something unique? Was it ultimately reactionary, fixated on the past, or quintessentially modern? What was the Third Reich's place in German history? How did it connect to prior epochs and successive phases? An enormous literature addresses such questions. This book, however, has focused largely on other central themes of Third Reich history. They include the contours of Hitler's increasingly personalized form of rule and its impact on how the Nazi state functioned; the extents and limits of coordination (i.e. nazification) of German society; the realities and illusions of the *Volksgemeinschaft*; the evolution of antisemitic policy and persecution, and transformations in the oppression of other outsiders; and insiders' knowledge about, and the level of their complicity in, Nazi crimes, whether as active perpetrators, spectators or otherwise 'implicated subjects'.[1] All these themes connect to an overarching question about how the Third Reich remained in power: Was it through coercion or consent? Immediately after the war, fuelled by the self-exculpatory stories Germans told and the Allies' emerging Cold War priorities, an image emerged of a population terrorized and brainwashed into submission by the Nazis. Decades later, the pendulum swung to the other side. In its extreme iteration, this latter view holds that the Third Reich was not maintained by force, but was a popular regime, a 'consensual dictatorship'; in other words, a 'self-policing society' rather than a police state, one that seduced and swayed beneficiaries rather than scaring them.[2] There is, however, no consensus. Some historians today sharply criticize arguments about widespread popular backing for Hitler, instead emphasizing fear and terror that 'loomed over everyone' to explain compliance.[3]

By addressing German responses to Hitler's regime, this book wades into the debate, but rather than taking sides, it takes a position that attempts, in light of recent scholarship, to balance both the approbatory and repressive aspects of Nazi Germany. It was not always either/or, but both/and. Coercion and consent were part of one another: the latter was inconceivable without the former, but terror itself also demanded approval. This symbiotic relationship between coercion and consent was only possible because the Nazis totally eliminated democratic norms and destroyed all liberal, democratic social and political organizations.

Approval generally leaves fewer traces in the historical record than do disputes and conflict. This is true for Nazi Germany as well. Most sources better show what concerned insider Germans and gave cause for complaint; far fewer reveal what they agreed with and admired. Nevertheless, there is now substantial and convincing evidence of support for much of the Nazis' programme among the majority German population. In significant numbers, they were broadly sympathetic with the Nazis' 'positive' goals of national and even racial rejuvenation. This, rewarded by Germany's success on the world stage and its initial wartime victories, coexisted with their support of the Nazi state for more pragmatic reasons, including the privileges of prosperity and power over others. However, consensus about the Nazis' negative goals – what had to be undermined, weakened and destroyed – was less fulsome and more fragmented. Fear and terror against insiders were deployed most viciously here, to crush any dissent over these objectives. The brutal, violent persecution of outsiders was, as we have seen, ubiquitous in Nazi Germany. Their fear was thus continuous, but its level and type varied over time. For example, Jewish Germans were first frightened about impoverishment; later they were afraid for their very lives. This book has addressed, in part, the recent call for a 'history of fear' under Hitler.[4]

It has become a truism in histories of Nazi Germany to note that compliance and conformity, or even compromise, should not be equated with consent; neither must accommodation mean agreement and approval. Such distinctions need further nuance. The former largely describes what Germans *did*, how they behaved, the latter what they *thought* and how they *felt* about it. In terms of their everyday conduct, Germans were generally united in going along with what the regime desired. By contrast, in terms of attitudes, opinions, inner convictions and motivations, there were 'multiple ambiguities' and a notable diversity. This latter point holds true about outsiders in Nazi Germany as well, but here we cannot speak of a 'community of action'.[5] Far greater variety typified their responses, though they shared, by their continued existence, a defiant stance towards the regime's ultimate aims. Germans who actively opposed the regime were exceedingly few; nonetheless, their brave commitment to ensuring that Nazi intentions were not wholly fulfilled deserves recognition.

When Hitler came to power in January 1933, he had three goals: the coordination of society to eliminate dissent and subject it to a single purpose, his own; exclusion of the Jews; and Germany's domination of Europe. With the achievement of the first and third, he extended the second to annihilation. He came perilously close to that goal. *Under the Swastika in Nazi Germany* has told five different stories within the framework created by those ambitions, considering the insiders on the one hand (the Nazis themselves, their accomplices and supporters) and outsiders (their victims and opponents) on the other. In a book of this length, certain subjects must remain out of focus. The aim has been to inspire readers to search out those stories themselves.

NOTES

PREFACE

1   Saul Friedländer, 'An Integrated History of the Holocaust: Some Methodological Challenges', in Dan Stone, ed. *The Holocaust and Historical Methodology* (New York: 2012).

INTRODUCTION

1   10 February 1933, in Max Domarus, ed. *Hitler: Speeches and Proclamations*, v.1 (Wauconda, IL: 1990), 245–50.
2   This book deliberately avoids repeated use of the usual term 'ordinary Germans' because it inadvertently suggests that other Germans – whether Jewish, Sinti and Roma, Black, homosexual, disabled or labelled 'asocial' – were not themselves ordinary and normal.

CHAPTER 1

1   Thomas Schaarschmidt, 'Multi-Level Governance in Hitler's Germany: Reassessing the Political Structure of the National Socialist State', *Historical Social Research / Historische Sozialforschung* 42, no. 2 (160) (2017): 218–42.
2   Hans Mommsen, 'Hitlers Stellung im nationalsozialistischen Herrschaftssystem', in Gerhard Hirschfeld and Lothar Kettenacker, eds., *Der Führerstaat. Mythos und Realität* (Stuttgart: 1981), 43–72.
3   Ian Kershaw, "Working towards the Führer': Reflections on the Nature of the Hitler Dictatorship', *Contemporary European History* 2, no. 2 (1993): 103–18. See also Ian Kershaw, *The 'Hitler Myth': Image and Reality in the Third Reich* (Oxford: 2001).
4   Theodore Abel, *The Nazi Movement*, 1st edn (New York: 1965), 288–9.

5   Jürgen Falter, *Hitlers Parteigenossen: Die Mitglieder der NSDAP 1919–1945* (Frankfurt am Main: 2020), 467–72.

6   Bastian Hein, *Elite für Volk und Führer? Die Allgemeine SS und ihre Mitglieder 1925–1945* (Munich: 2012), 123–30.

7   Daniel Siemens, *Stormtroopers: A New History of Hitler's Brownshirts* (New Haven, CT: 2017), 142.

8   Thomas Kühne, *Belonging and Genocide: Hitler's Community, 1918–1945* (New Haven, CT: 2010), 143.

9   Michael H. Kater, *Hitler Youth* (Cambridge, MA: 2004), 20.

10 Kühne, 'Belonging and Genocide', 143.

11 Claudia Koonz, *The Nazi Conscience* (Cambridge, MA: 2003), 133.

12 Nikolaus Wachsmann, *Hitler's Prisons: Legal Terror in Nazi Germany* (New Haven, CT: 2004), 71.

13 Thomas Childers, *The Third Reich: A History of Nazi Germany* (New York: 2017), 221.

14 Wachsmann, *Hitler's Prisons*, 388; Ingo Müller, *Hitler's Justice: The Courts of the Third Reich*, trans. Deborah Lucas Schneider (Cambridge, MA: 1991), 73.

15 Peter Hayes, 'German Big Business and the National Revolution, 1933–34', in Hermann Beck and Larry Eugene Jones, eds. *Weimar to Hitler: Studies in the Dissolution of the Weimar Republic and the Establishment of the Third Reich, 1932–1934* (New York: 2019), 142.

16 Peter Hayes, *Industry and Ideology: IG Farben in the Nazi Era* (Cambridge, UK: 2001), 102–3.

17 Ralf Banken, 'Introduction: The Room for Manoeuvre for Firms in the Third Reich', *Business History* 62, no. 3 (2020): 375–92.

18 Jeremy Noakes, 'German Conservatives and the Third Reich: An Ambiguous Relationship', in Martin Blinkhorn, ed. *Fascists and Conservatives: The Radical Right and the Establishment in Twentieth-Century Europe* (London: 1990), 89.

19 Shelley Baranowski, 'Conservative Elite Anti-Semitism from the Weimar Republic to the Third Reich', *German Studies Review* 19, no. 3 (1996), 527.

20 Ben H. Shepherd, *Hitler's Soldiers: The German Army in the Third Reich* (New Haven, CT: 2016), xxiii.

21 Falter, *Hitlers Parteigenossen*, 73–6.

22 Peter Fritzsche, *Hitler's First Hundred Days: When Germans Embraced the Third Reich* (New York: 2020), 212.

23 Detlev K. Peukert, 'Working-Class Resistance: Problems and Options', in David Clay Large, ed. *Contending with Hitler: Varieties of German Resistance in the Third Reich* (Cambridge: 1991), 43.

24 David Welch, 'Nazi Propaganda and the Volksgemeinschaft: Constructing a People's Community', *Journal of Contemporary History* 39, no. 2 (2004): 226.

25   Alf Lüdtke, 'The Appeal of Exterminating "Others": German Workers and the Limits of Resistance', *Journal of Modern History* 64 (1992): S46-67.

26   Richard Evans, *The Third Reich in Power* (London: 2005), 440.

27   Michael Wildt, 'Self-Reassurance in Troubled Times: German Diaries during the Upheavals of 1933', in Alf Lüdtke, ed. *Everyday Life in Mass Dictatorship: Collusion and Evasion* (Basingstoke: 2016), 59-60.

28   Claudia Koonz, *Mothers in the Fatherland: Women, the Family and Nazi Politics* (London: 1986), 144, 183.

29   Ibid., xxii.

30   Ute Frevert, *Women in German History: From Bourgeois Emancipation to Sexual Liberation*, trans. Stuart McKinnon-Evans (Oxford: 1989), 252.

31   William John Wilson, 'Festivals in the Third Reich' (PhD diss., McMaster University, 1994), 116.

32   Manfred Gailus, 'Religion', in Shelley Baranowski, Armin Nolzen and Claus-Christian W. Szejnmann, eds. *A Companion to Nazi Germany* (Hoboken, NJ: 2018), 337-8.

33   Peter Lambert, 'The Third Reich: Police State or Self-Policing Society?' in Alf Lüdtke, ed. *Everyday Life in Mass Dictatorships: Collusion and Evasion* (Houndmills: 2016), 43.

34   Koonz, *Conscience*, 190-1.

35   Jane Caplan and Nikolaus Wachsmann, eds. 'Introduction', in *Concentration Camps in Nazi Germany: The New Histories* (London: 2010), 2.

36   Fritzsche, *Hitler's First Hundred Days*, 285.

37   Jürgen Matthäus et al., *Jewish Responses to Persecution*, vol. 1, 1933-8 (Lanham, MD: 2010), xvii.

38   Margarete Limberg and Hubert Ruebsaat, eds. *Germans No More: Accounts of Jewish Everyday Life*, trans. Alan Nothnagle (New York: 2006), 11.

39   Wolf Gruner, 'Indifference? Participation and Protest as Individual Responses to the Persecution of the Jews as Revealed in Berlin Police Logs and Trial Records, 1933-45', in Susanna Schrafstetter and Alan E. Steinweis, eds. *The Germans and the Holocaust: Popular Responses to the Persecution and Murder of the Jews* (New York: 2015), 62.

40   Limberg and Ruebsaat, *Germans No More*, 103-4.

41   Ibid., 79.

42   Evans, *Third Reich in Power*, 508-9.

43   Alan R. Rushton, *Talking Back against the Nazi Scheme to Kill the Handicapped Citizens of Germany 1933-1945* (Newcastle: 2018), 46.

44   Nikolaus Wachsmann, 'From Indefinite Confinement to Extermination: "Habitual Criminals" in the Third Reich', in Robert Gellatelyand Nathan Stoltzfus, eds. *Social Outsiders in Nazi Germany* (Princeton, NJ: 2001), 170, 173.

45   Michael Burleigh and Wolfgang Wippermann, *The Racial State: Germany 1933–1945* (Cambridge: 1991), 183.

46   Wayne Geerling and Gary Magee, *Quantifying Resistance: Political Crime and the People's Court in Nazi Germany* (Singapore: 2017).

47   Christian Goeschel and Nikolaus Wachsmann, eds. *The Nazi Concentration Camps, 1933–1939: A Documentary History* (Lincoln: University of Nebraska Press, 2012), xv.

48   Richard Evans, *The Coming of the Third Reich* (London: 2003), 359–60.

49   Burleigh and Wippermann, *Racial State*, 138–9.

50   Doris Bergen, *Twisted Cross: The German Christian Movement in the Third Reich* (Chapel Hill, NC: 1996), 7.

51   Christopher J. Probst, *Demonizing the Jews: Luther and the Protestant Church in Nazi Germany* (Bloomington, IN: 2012), 89.

52   Rushton, *Talking Back*, 47.

53   Gisela Bock, 'Antinatalism, Maternity and Paternity in National Socialist Racism', in David F. Crew, ed. *Nazism and German Society 1933–1945* (New York: 1994), 117.

54   Gordon Thomas and Greg Lewis, *Defying Hitler: The Germans Who Resisted Nazi Rule* (New York: 2019), 49.

55   Marion A. Kaplan, *Between Dignity and Despair: Jewish Life in Nazi Germany* (New York: 1998), 46.

56   'Jüdischer Kulturbund', Jewish Virtual Library, https://www.jewishvir tuallibrary.org/juedischer-kulturbund (accessed 15 June 2022).

CHAPTER 2

1   Milan Hauner, *Hitler: A Chronology of His Life and Time*, 2nd edn (Basingstoke: 2008), 120.

2   The remainder belonged to the SS combat arm, the precursor to the Waffen-SS. Figures from Hein, *Elite für Volk und Führer?*, 1, 205, 308, 260.

3   R. J. Overy, *Goering: The 'Iron Man'* (London: 1984), 68.

4   Jeremy Noakes, 'Viceroys of the Reich: *Gauleiters* 1925–45', in Anthony McElligott and Tim Kirk, eds. *Working towards the Führer: Essays in Honour of Sir Ian Kershaw* (Manchester: 2003), 132.

5   Jeremy Noakes, 'Leaders of the People? The Nazi Party and German Society', *Journal of Contemporary History* 39, no. 2 (2004): 203.

6   Arnd Krüger, '"Once the Olympics are through, we'll beat up the Jew": German Jewish Sport 1898–1938 and the Anti-Semitic Discourse', *Journal of Sport History* 26, no. 2 (1999): 353–75.

7   Michael Kater, *Doctors under Hitler* (Chapel Hill, NC: 1989), 55–7.

8   Ulrich Herbert, 'Good Times, Bad Times: Memories of the Third Reich', in Richard Bessel, ed. *Life in the Third Reich* (Oxford: 1987).

9   Evans, *Third Reich in Power*, 635.

10   Ian Kershaw, *Popular Opinion and Political Dissent in the Third Reich: Bavaria 1933–1945* (Oxford: 1983), 95.

11   Ibid., 90.

12   Ibid., 64.

13   Jill Stephenson, 'Women's Labor Service in Nazi Germany', *Central European History* 15, no. 3 (1982): 255.

14   Lisa Pine, Family and the Third Reich (PhD Thesis, London School of Economics and Political Science, 1996), 59.

15   Shepherd, *Hitler's Soldiers*.

16   Siegfried Knappe, *Soldat: Reflections of a German Soldier, 1936–1949* (New York: 1992), 100.

17   Shepherd, *Hitler's Soldiers*, 14.

18   Caplan and Wachsmann, 'Introduction', 18–21.

19   Paul Moore, 'German Popular Opinion on the Nazi Concentration Camps, 1933–1939' (PhD Thesis, Birkbeck College, University of London, 2010), 235.

20   Otto Dov Kulka and Eberhard Jäckel, eds. *The Jews in the Secret Nazi Reports on Popular Opinion in Germany, 1933–1945*, trans. William Templar (New Haven, CT: 2010), 223.

21   Thomas A. Kohut, *A German Generation: An Experiential History of the Twentieth Century* (New Haven, CT: 2012), 136.

22   Avraham Barkai, *From Boycott to Annihilation: The Economic Struggle of German Jews, 1933*–1943, trans. William Templar (Hanover, NH: 1989), 125–6.

23   Dorothea Buck, '70 Years of Coercion in German Psychiatric Institutions, Experienced and Witnessed', keynote lecture, World Psychiatric Organisation Congress, Dresden, Germany, 6–8 June 2007, http://www.bpe-online.de/1/buck-wpa-2007-e.pdf (accessed 15 June 2022).

24   'Otto Rosenberg', Holocaust Memorial Day Trust, https://www.hmd.org.uk/wp-content/uploads/old-images/otto_rosenberg_life_story_hmd.pdf (accessed 15 June 2022).

25   Hans J. Massaquoi, *Destined to Witness: Growing Up Black in Nazi Germany* (New York: 1999), 100.

26   Tina M. Campt, *Other Germans: Black Germans and the Politics of Race, Gender, and Memory in the Third Reich* (Ann Arbor, MI: 2004), 73.

27   Günter Grau, *Hidden Holocaust?: Gay and Lesbian Persecution in Germany 1933–45* (London: 1995), 117.

28 Detlef Schmiechen-Ackermann, 'Resistance', in Shelley Baranowski, Armin Nolzen and Claus-Christian W. Szejnmann, eds. *A Companion to Nazi Germany* (Hoboken, NJ: 2018), 130.

29 Kershaw, *Popular Opinion*, 202.

30 Detlef Garbe, *Between Resistance and Martyrdom: Jehovah's Witnesses in the Third Reich*, trans. Dagmar G. Grimm (Madison, WI: 2008), 246, 480.

31 Kater, *Hitler Youth*, 23.

32 David Welch, *The Third Reich: Politics and Propaganda*, 2nd edn (London: 2002), 78.

33 Geerling and Magee, *Quantifying Resistance*, 67.

34 Matthäus and Roseman, *Jewish Responses*, 241.

35 Claudia Koonz, 'Ethical Dilemmas and Nazi Eugenics: Single-Issue Dissent in Religious Contexts', *Journal of Modern History* 64 (1992): S25.

CHAPTER 3

1 Ian Kershaw, *Hitler, 1936–1945: Nemesis* (London: 2000), 252.

2 Peter Longerich, *Goebbels: A Biography*, trans. Alan Bance, Jeremy Noakes and Lesley Sharpe. (London: 2015), 400.

3 Jürgen Matthäus, Jochen Böhler and Klaus-Michael Mallmann, *War, Pacification, and Mass Murder, 1939: The Einsatzgruppen in Poland* (Lanham, MD: 2014), 52.

4 Armin Nolzen, 'The NSDAP after 1933: Members, Positions, Technologies, Interactions', in Shelley Baranowski, Armin Nolzen and Claus-Christian W. Szejnmann, eds. *A Companion to Nazi Germany* (Hoboken, NJ: 2018), 100.

5 Noakes, 'Leaders', 209.

6 Peter Hayes, 'The Economy', in Robert Gellately, ed. *The Oxford Illustrated History of the Third Reich* (Oxford: 2018), 201.

7 Julia Torrie, 'The Home Front', in Robert Gellately, ed. *The Oxford Illustrated History of the Third Reich* (Oxford: 2018), 287.

8 Richard Overy, 'The German Home Front under the Bombs', in Shelley Baranowski, Armin Nolzen and Claus-Christian W. Szejnmann, eds. *A Companion to Nazi Germany* (Hoboken, NJ: 2018), 232.

9 Kristin Semmens, *Seeing Hitler's Germany: Tourism in the Third Reich* (Basingstoke: 2005), 157.

10 Knappe, *Soldat*, 190; Gerhardt B. Thamm, *Boy Soldier: A German Teenager at the Nazi Twilight* (Jefferson, NC: 2000), 23.

11   Hayes, 'The Economy', 203.

12   Irmtraud Heike, 'Female Concentration Camp Guards as Perpetrators: Three Case Studies', in Olaf Jensen and Claus-Christian W. Szejnmann, eds. *Ordinary People as Mass Murderers: Perpetrators in Comparative Perspectives* (Basingstoke: 2008), 125.

13   Rushton, *Talking Back*, 76.

14   Knappe, *Soldat*, 149.

15   Statistics for German casualties differ widely. This estimate is derived from Rüdiger Overmans, *Deutsche militärische Verluste im Zweiten Weltkrieg* (Oldenbourg: 2000).

16   Limberg and Ruebsaat, *Germans No More*, 151.

17   Siemens, *Stormtroopers*, 197.

18   Alan E. Steinweis, *Kristallnacht 1938* (Cambridge, MA: 2009), 5–6.

19   Wolf Gruner, '"Worse than Vandals": The Mass Destruction of Jewish Homes and Jewish Responses during the 1938 Pogrom', in Steven J. Ross, et al., eds. *New Perspectives on Kristallnacht: After 80 Years, the Nazi Pogrom in Global Comparison* (Lafayette, IN: 2019), 28–9.

20   Uta Gerhardt and Thomas Karlauf, eds. *The Night of Broken Glass: Eyewitness Accounts of Kristallnacht*, trans. Robert Simmons and Nick Somers (Cambridge, UK: 2012), 106.

21   Kaplan, *Between Dignity and Despair*, 24.

22   Nicholas Stargardt, *Witnesses of War: Children's Lives under the Nazis* (London: 2005), 28.

23   Rushton, *Talking Back*, 107.

24   Sarah Helm, *If This Is a Woman: Inside Ravensbrück – Hitler's Concentration Camp for Women* (London: 2015), 96.

25   Marc Buggeln, 'Unfree and Forced Labour', in Shelley Baranowski, Armin Nolzen and Claus-Christian W. Szejnmann, eds. *A Companion to Nazi Germany* (Hoboken, NJ: 2018), 520.

26   'Dietrich Bonhoeffer: The Church and the Jewish Question', United States Holocaust Memorial Museum, https://www.ushmm.org/informat ion/exhibitions/online-exhibitions/special-focus/dietrich-bonhoeffer/ church-and-jewish-question (accessed 15 June 2022).

27   Wolf Gruner, *'Impudent Jews': Forgotten Stories of Individual Jewish Resistance in Hitler's Germany* (New Haven, CT: 2023).

CHAPTER 4

1   Klaus H. Schmider, *Hitler's Fatal Miscalculation: Why Germany Declared War on the United States* (Cambridge: 2021).

2   Kershaw, *Hitler, 1936–1945: Nemesis*, 604.

3   Kühne, *Belonging and Genocide*, 1.

4   Siemens, *Stormtroopers*, 266.

5   Overy, *Goering*, 205.

6   Kershaw, *Hitler, 1936–1945: Nemesis*, 511.

7   Ibid., 391.

8   Ulrich Herbert, *Hitler's Foreign Workers: Enforced Foreign Labour in Germany under the Third Reich*, trans. William Templar (Cambridge: 1997).

9   Peter Hayes, 'Industry under the Swastika', in Harold James and Jakob Tanner, eds. *Enterprise in the Period of Fascism in Europe*, 1st edn (London: 2002), 35.

10 Richard Evans, *The Third Reich at War* (London: 2008), 609.

11 Rushton, *Talking Back*, 216.

12 Earl R. Beck, 'Under the Bombs', in Martin Middlebrook and Igor Primoratz, eds. *Terror from the Sky: The Bombing of German Cities in World War II* (New York: 2010), 64.

13 Nicholas Stargardt, *The German War: A Nation under Arms, 1939–45* (London: 2015), 375–80.

14 Ibid., 379.

15 Karen Hagemann, 'Mobilizing Women for War: The History, Historiography, and Memory of German Women's War Service in the Two World Wars', *Journal of Military History* 75, no. 4 (2011): 1079–80.

16 Knappe, *Soldat*, 213.

17 Kühne, *Belonging and Genocide*, 107.

18 Christopher R. Browning, *Ordinary Men: Reserve Police Battalion 101 and the Final Solution in Poland* (New York: 1993), xv.

19 Kaplan, *Dignity and Despair*, 157.

20 Rushton, *Talking Back*, 227.

21 Massaquoi, *Destined to Witness*, 232.

22 Richard N. Lutjens Jr., *Submerged on the Surface: The Not-So-Hidden Jews of Nazi Berlin, 1941–1945* (New York: 2019), 16, 33.

CHAPTER 5

1   By the end of the war, membership had reached nine million (Falter, *Hitlers Parteigenossen*, 59–60, 104).

2   Stargardt, *The German War*, 455.

3   Ian Kershaw, *The End: The Defiance and Destruction of Hitler's Germany, 1944–1945* (New York: 2011), 398.

4   Kershaw, *The End*, 225.

5   Ibid., 31.
6   Semmens, *Seeing Hitler's Germany*, 163.
7   Kershaw, *The End*, 220.
8   Stargardt, *The German War*, 487.
9   Friedländer, 'Integrated History', 183.
10   Stargardt, *The German War*, 474.
11   Christian Goeschel, *Suicide in Nazi Germany* (Oxford: 2009), 160.
12   This was my maternal grandmother's experience. In autumn 1944, eighteen-year-old Katharina Kühbauch fled her village near Belgrade, Serbia. She worked on an Austrian farm until the war ended.
13   Sven Keller, 'Total Defeat: War, Society, and Violence in the Last Year of National Socialism', in Shelley Baranowski, Armin Nolzen and Claus-Christian W. Szejnmann, eds. *A Companion to Nazi Germany* (Hoboken, NJ: 2018), 256.
14   Winfried Heinemann, *Operation 'Valkyrie': A Military History of the 20 July 1944 Plot* (Munich: 2022), 173.
15   Daniel Fraenkel, 'The German Righteous among the Nations', Yad Vashem, https://www.yadvashem.org/righteous/resources/the-german-righteous-among-the-nations.html (accessed 15 June 2022).

CONCLUSION

1   Michael Rothberg, *The Implicated Subject: Beyond Victims and Perpetrators* (Stanford, CA: 2019).
2   Frank Bajohr, ' "Consensual Dictatorship" (*Zustimmungsdiktatur*) and "Community of the People" (*Volksgemeinschaft*): Some Reflections on the Interaction between Nazi State and German Society in the Persecution of the Jews after 1933', *Politeja* 14 (2010): 521–6; Lambert, 'The Third Reich: Police State or Self-Policing Society?'.
3   Evans, *Third Reich in Power*, 117.
4   Nazi Terror, FORUM, *German History* 29, no. 1 (2011): 92.
5   Detlev Peukert, *Inside Nazi Germany: Conformity, Opposition and Racism in Everyday Life*, trans. Richard Deveson (New Haven, CT: 1987), 243; Frank Bajohr, ' "Community of Action" and Diversity of Attitudes', in Martina Steber and Bernhard Gotto, eds. *Visions of Community in Nazi Germany: Social Engineering and Private Lives* (Oxford: 2014), 188.

SELECTED FURTHER READING

Beck, Hermann, and Larry Eugene Jones, eds. *From Weimar to Hitler: Studies in the Dissolution of the Weimar Republic and the Establishment of the Third Reich, 1932–1934* (New York: 2019).

Benz, Wolfgang, and Walter H. Pehle, eds. *Encyclopedia of Resistance to the Nazi Movement*, trans. Lance W. Garmer (New York: 1997).

Browning, Christopher R. *The Origins of the Final Solution: The Evolution of Nazi Jewish Policy, September 1939–March 1942* (Lincoln, NE: 2004).

Chapoutot, Johann. *The Law of Blood: Thinking and Acting as a Nazi* (Cambridge, MA: 2018).

Dams, Carsten, and Michael Stolle. *The Gestapo: Power and Terror in the Third Reich* (Oxford: 2014).

Eley, Geoffrey. N*azism as Fascism: Violence, Ideology, and the Grounds of Consent 1930–1945* (London: 2013).

Ericksen, Robert P. *Complicity in the Holocaust: Churches and Universities in Nazi Germany* (Cambridge: 2012).

Föllmer, Moritz. *Culture in the Third Reich*, trans. Jeremy Noakes and Lesley Sharpe (Oxford: 2020).

Gellately, Robert. *Hitler's True Believers: How Ordinary People Became Nazis* (Oxford: 2020).

Gruner, Wolf, and Jörg Osterloh, eds. *The Greater German Reich and the Jews: Nazi Persecution in the Annexed Territories 1935–1945* (New York: 2017).

Harvey, Elizabeth, and Johannes Hürter, eds. *Hitler: New Research* (Berlin: 2018).

Harvey, Elizabeth, Johannes Hürter, Maiken Umbach and Andreas Wirsching, eds. *Private Life and Privacy in Nazi Germany* (Cambridge: 2019).

Hayes, Peter. *Why? Explaining the Holocaust* (New York: 2017).

Ingrao, Christian. *The Promise of the East: Nazi Hopes and Genocide 1939–1943* (Medford, MA: 2019).

Jarausch, Konrad H. *Broken Lives: How Ordinary Germans Experienced the Twentieth Century* (Princeton, NJ: 2018).

Selected Further Reading

Johnson, Eric A., and Karl-Heinz Reuband, eds. *What We Knew: Terror, Mass Murder, and Everyday Life in Nazi Germany – An Oral History* (Cambridge, MA: 2005).

Kaplan, Thomas Pegelow, and Wolf Gruner, eds. *Resisting Persecution: Jews and Their Petitions during the Holocaust* (New York: 2020).

Kreutzmüller, Christoph, and Jonathan R. Zatlin, eds. *Dispossession: Plundering German Jewry, 1933–1953* (Ann Arbor, MI: 2020).

Lewy, Guenter. *Nazi Persecution of the Gypsies* (Oxford: 1999).

Overy, Richard. *The Third Reich: A Chronicle* (London: 2010).

Pendas, Devin O., Mark Roseman and Richard F. Wetzell, eds. *Beyond the Racial State: Rethinking Nazi Germany* (Cambridge: 2017).

Pine, Lisa, ed. *Life and Times in Nazi Germany* (London: 2016).

Rabinbach, Anson, and Sander L. Gilman, eds. *The Third Reich Sourcebook* (Berkeley, CA: 2013).

Robertson, Michael, Edwina Light and Astrid Ley. *The First into the Dark: The Nazi Persecution of the Disabled* (Broadway, Australia: 2019).

Schrafstetter, Susanna, and Alan E. Steinweis, eds. *The Germans and the Holocaust: Popular Responses to the Persecution and Murder of the Jews* (New York: 2015).

Steinweis, Alan E., and Robert D. Rachlin, eds. *The Law in Nazi Germany: Ideology, Opportunism, and the Perversion of Justice* (New York: 2013).

Stoltzfus, Nathan. *Hitler's Compromises: Coercion and Consensus in Nazi Germany* (New Haven, CT: 2016).

Süß, Dietmar. *Death from the Skies: How the British and Germans Survived Bombing in World War II* (Oxford: 2014).

Timpe, Julia. *Nazi-Organized Recreation and Entertainment in the Third Reich* (London: 2017).

Tooze, Adam. *The Wages of Destruction: The Making and Breaking of the Nazi Economy* (New York: 2006).

Wachsmann, Nikolaus. *KL: A History of the Nazi Concentration Camps* (New York: 2015).

Weale, Adrian. *The SS: A New History* (London: 2010).

Wildt, Michael. *Uncompromising Generation: The Nazi Leadership of the Reich Security Main Office* (Madison, WI: 2010).

Wünschmann, Kim. *Before Auschwitz: Jewish Prisoners in the Prewar Concentration Camps* (Cambridge, MA: 2015).

INDEX

Index

Index

Index

Index

Index

Index

Index

Index